Portraits of Christ

HENRY GARIEPY

Devotional Studies of the Names of Jesus

Fleming H. Revell Company
Old Tappan, New Jersey

All Scripture quotations in this volume unless otherwise indicated are from the King James Version of the Bible.

Scripture quotations marked NEB are from The New English Bible. © The Delegates of the Oxford University Press and the Syndics of the Cambridge University Press 1961 and 1970. Reprinted by permission.

Scripture quotations marked RSV are from the Revised Standard Version of the Bible. Copyrighted 1946 and 1952.

The Amplified New Testament, By permission of the Lockman Foundation.

Scripture quotations marked MOFFATT are from THE BIBLE: A NEW TRANSLATION by James Moffatt. Copyright, 1954 by James Moffatt. By permission of Harper & Row, Publishers, Inc.

Excerpts in the *Portrait* titled "Lord" are from *The Greek-English Lexicon* by W. F. Arndt and F. W. Gingrich, published by Walter de Gruyter & Company, Berlin, Germany.

Library of Congress Cataloging in Publication Data

Gariepy, Henry.
    Portraits of Christ.

1. Jesus Christ—Name—meditations. I. Title.
BT590.N2G28   232   73-15903
ISBN 0-8007-0644-7

Copyright © 1974 by The Salvation Army
Published by Fleming H. Revell Company
All rights reserved
Printed in the United States of America

Dedicated to
Marjorie
My partner and companion in
life's greatest adventure—
endeavoring to discover and
follow Jesus Christ

Contents

	Foreword	7
	Introduction	9
I	The Prophecy	15
II	The Advent	45
III	The Person	55
IV	The Ministry	77

Foreword

The decade of the seventies may well be remembered as the years during which the world saw increased prominence given to the Person and work of the Lord Jesus Christ. In the Jesus People, we have been encouraged to see multitudes of young people captured by Christ, without necessarily endorsing their life-style. Tens of thousands of congregations distributed over fifty million Gospels as part of the Key 73 objective to call the continent to Christ. The portrayals of Christ through secular drama have often been incomplete and distorted—perhaps irreverent—but they have set millions of unchurched minds thinking of the Redeemer. There is a current renaissance of interest in the Second Coming of Christ—a scriptural assurance too long neglected.

To whatever extent these developments have helped to turn men's hearts to Christ, to bring the unchurched to personal redemption, to lift up Christ to the world, to reveal Him as crucified and resurrected Saviour—to that extent these developments must be considered as motivated by the Holy Spirit in our day. Jesus Himself declared of the Holy Spirit, "He shall glorify Me."

Major Henry Gariepy has done us all a service by leading us into a deeper understanding of the unfathomable dimensions of Christ's Person and work. Each of the names by which He has been called shows new facet of His life, His ministry, and His relevance to our contemporary needs.

The Holy Spirit, who "guides us into all truth," will use these devotional messages to challenge us to be worthy representatives of Christ in our circle of influence. He calls for "bright and morning stars" to light the darkness and bring the promise of dawn. He needs "good shepherds" to watch over both lambs and sheep, and to search diligently for the lost and fallen of the flock. To the unsavory wastelands of life we must bring the fragrance of the "lily of the valley" and the "rose of Sharon." We all share with Him the title "son of man." Through His redeeming power we are privileged also to bear the name "son of God,"—". . . as many as received him, to them gave he power to become the sons of God."

If this volume leads the people of God to be more Christlike, within the limitations of our own humanity, then the Holy Spirit will have achieved His purpose in our lives through Major Gariepy's thoughtful expositions.

COLONEL JOHN D. WALDRON

Introduction

"What's in a name?" To this question posed by Shakespeare, today we would have to answer, "Not very much." Today a name is selected for its association with a loved one or person admired, or perhaps because of its euphonious quality. A name has become, for the most part, a label of identification.

That was not always so. In biblical times, a name had a very significant connotation. Often a name would denote some important characteristic of the person, or something related to the history of the person or his time.

Sometimes a person's name was changed to indicate the change of character or an epochal event in his history. Such was the case when God changed Abram's name to Abraham (Genesis 17:5). In the great covenant God entered into with Abram, the new name signified *Father of a multitude* or *exalted father*. Jacob's name meant *supplanter* and aptly described his early life. But in his spiritually traumatic experience at Peniel, his name was changed to *Israel* to signify that as a spiritual prince he had power with God. Moses changed Oshea's name to Joshua which meant *salvation* and prophetically spoke of his work in delivering Israel from her enemies (Numbers 13:16). Isaiah gave to his two sons symbolic names relating to his prophecies to Israel (Isaiah 7:3; 8:3).

Jesus beautifully prophesied the sturdy qualities to be developed in the big fisherman He recruited as a disciple when He changed his name from Simon which meant *shifting sand* to Cephas or Peter, meaning *rock* (John 1:42). Saul had such a transforming experience on the Damascus Road that his name as well as his nature was changed.

One of God's greatest revelations was memorialized in a name. The name Methuselah meant, in essence, *when he is gone it shall be sent.* His name prophesied the Deluge. What a testimony to God's grace and forebearance that the one whose life span was to measure the length of opportunity man had to repent and be spared destruction was the longest life lived upon earth.

Thus, in those days, names were often very significant, and sometimes sacred.

It was not too long ago that our Anglo-Saxon names were assigned for significant denotation. Patronymic names indicated lineage, for example, Johnson, Ericson, Peterson, et cetera. Occupations were often indicated in names such as Smith, Miller, Carpenter. Thus a name often gave a *prima facie* knowledge about the person.

Goethe speaks of a name being inseparable from a person:

> A man's name is not like a mantle which merely hangs about him . . . but a perfectly fitting garment, which, like the skin, has grown over him, at which one cannot rake and scrape without injuring the man himself.

But of all the names in history, none are so significant, so sacred, so sublime and superlative as the names of Jesus. Paul in his great Christological passage exclaims, "God has given Him a name which is above every name" (*see* Philippians 2:9). Many inspired hymnodists caught the theme and penned immortal words which have found an honored place in our hymnbooks.

Throughout the Old and New Testaments, one finds a little over one hundred names and titles for Jesus Christ, gleaming like jewels with radiance and luster. One of the objects of this writing is to take these coruscating gems and attempt to set them in a diadem of devotional study so that our lives may be further brightened and our hearts illumined by their shining truths. In adhering to the restriction of space, the number of titles selected correspond to the number of weeks in a year. For many, this may facilitate the devotional use of this writing.

After I had embarked on this intriguing Bible study, the question posed itself to me, "Why are there so many names and titles for Christ?" No other personage of history seems to have more than one main title, for example Alexander the Great, William the Conqueror, Washington the Father of His Country. But Jesus Christ had over one hundred names and titles. Why this polynomial quality of our Lord?

Is it not because although a name is descriptive it is also restrictive? It states that a person is this or not that. A name or a title has a self-imposed limitation and no one could begin to describe or define Jesus Christ. In one sense, He is the Unnameable One. His glory and His greatness defy description and definition.

One of the best ways to know and understand Christ is to perceive the portrait that is put together by the mosaic of names and titles revealed in Scripture. Each name and title reveals some unique aspect of His person and His purpose. These names and titles are an index to the nature of Christ.

Thus a study of the names and titles of Christ can prove most salutary to the Christian. May this study lead us to know Christ better, and knowing Him to love Him, and loving Him to serve Him and reveal His love and power to a world in crisis.

I
The Prophecy

Old Testament Names and Titles Prophetically Ascribed

1. Seed of the Woman
2. Shiloh
3. Redeemer
4. Lily of the Valley
5. Wonderful Counselor
6. The Mighty God
7. The Everlasting Father
8. The Prince of Peace
9. Rod and Branch
10. Man of Sorrows
11. Messiah
12. King
13. Messenger of the Covenant
14. Sun of Righteousness

Portrait 1

Seed of the Woman

And I will put enmity . . . between thy seed and her seed: it shall bruise thy head, and thou shalt bruise his heel.

Genesis 3:15

The only Utopia ever known to man on earth was the idyllic setting of the Garden of Eden. There Adam and Eve basked in perfect splendor. They had beauty, peace, perfection of body and mind, the companionship of each other, and a sense of divine presence. They were a fresh thought from the mind of God. They were a fresh breath from the Spirit of God. They were made in the very likeness of their Creator.

They had everything going for them. Then suddenly—disaster! The Fall! By disbelief and disobedience they fell from their pinnacle of paradise. The sky blackened over their lives. They became sinners, transgressors against their mighty and loving Creator. The venom of sin entered the bloodstream of humanity. Paradise became lost. The sentence of death was pronounced.

Suddenly in that awful dark sky there appears the twinkling of a star—the star of prophetical promise. There is the promise of the seed of the woman. She would have offspring. God's creation would not be aborted. There would come from that offspring the conquest of Satan and sin: "It shall bruise thy head." A deathblow would be dealt to the head of sin.

Thus the "seed of the woman" was the first messianic reference and promise given to man. It was the lone star on man's horizon in the dawn of creation by which he would steer his frail bark of life toward a haven of hope. It was the first title of a promised Deliverer from The Fall and its consequences. It prophesied His victorious battle on behalf of creation.

This title also suggests, and many scholars aver that it prophesies, the virgin birth of Jesus Christ. In the Old Testament, genealogy is reckoned through the man and not the woman. This reference to Christ being the seed of a woman is in keeping with the fact that He would not have earthly paternity.

The doctrine of the virgin birth has been a battlefield of theological controversy through the years. Biologically, a virgin birth is an impossibility, but so was the raising of Lazarus and the Resurrection. Someone has stated, "The presence of mystery is the footprint of the divine." In harmony with God's miraculous power, the virgin birth would be but one of a chain of supernatural events in the marvelous life and mission of our Lord.

O Christ, my Saviour from the dawn of creation, I am awed by the mystery and the majesty that brought You from eternity down to man. Such a divine love overwhelms me.

Portrait 2

Shiloh

The sceptre shall not depart from Judah, nor a lawgiver from between his feet, until Shiloh come; and unto him shall the gathering of the people be.

Genesis 49:10

This title comes to us from the poem and prophecy of the aged patriarch Jacob who, on his deathbed, speaks to each of his sons. As we read Jacob's pronouncements of blessings, we find scathing rebuke where there had been moral failure. Reuben, who by virtue of being the firstborn should have the greatest blessing, is described as having been "unstable as water." Simeon and Levi are said to have had "instruments of cruelty in their habitations." By their instability and unbridled lust and cruelty, they forfeited the privileges of their birthright. As we read on, we find that the signal blessings are reserved for the tribes of Judah and Joseph.

In the blessing pronounced upon the tribe of Judah, we suddenly see another piece of the mosaic of messianic prophecy. First, in Genesis, it was "the seed," then to Abraham it was "thy seed," and now the very tribe is revealed out of which will come the Messiah.

In that prophecy, we have this cryptic name *Shiloh*. It comes from a verb signifying *to rest.* Thus it is prophetical of the rest and peace which Jesus gives to His followers. In this war-haunted world, there are millions to whom this title should give reassurance. He is able to give an inward peace and equilibrium amidst the disquietude and turmoil of the outward world.

In Paris, I observed on the Rue de la Paix, the Street of Peace, a towering and ornamented monument of Napoleon. It seemed incongruous that this man of war and bloodshed should be so prominently positioned over the Street of Peace. Jesus Christ towers over the centuries of strife and bloodshed as the only One who can give true rest and peace.

In our country, there is a place in Tennessee with this beautiful name of Shiloh, meaning *rest*. However, it is known only as a place of bloodshed. Our encyclopedias, dictionaries, and history books define it as a battlefield of the Civil War where twenty-five thousand men were mortally wounded. The events are far removed from the meaning of its name.

Jesus Christ is true to the meaning of each of His great titles. They are all in perfect keeping with His character and mission. He is the only One who will bring rest to His people. Just as He stilled the storm-tossed and troubled waters of the Sea of Galilee, so He will still the squalls and storms that would disrupt our lives and our peace. He is the One who promised to all who would come to Him, "I will give you rest."

O Christ, still the restlessness of my heart and give me the power of Thy peace.

Portrait 3
Redeemer

For I know that my redeemer liveth, and that he shall stand at the latter day upon the earth.

Job 19:25

From Job, the Shakespeare of the Old Testament, we have this textual jewel. It shines all the brighter because of its night-enshrouded setting. Job had experienced in quick succession the loss of his possessions and health, the reproof of his wife, and the suspicion of his friends. He could well have become the world's greatest pessimist. Instead we see him giving the classic example of positive thinking in a negative situation—"I know that my Redeemer liveth."

These words were a lofty climax to the speeches of Job. They are words enshrined in the heart of every believer. Repeated over innumerable graves, they have given hope and reassurance. They incorporate the message that is most needed in the world today—Christ is vibrantly alive. Also that He is the spaceman extraordinary who will someday make His reentry into our troubled and tortured world in the grand denouement of creation.

What did this word *redeemer* mean when uttered by Job? The Hebrew word *goel* represented the kinsman whose duty it was to recover a captured or enslaved relative.

We were captives of sin and Satan. As our spiritual Kinsman, Jesus delivered us from this enslavement and made us free.

This word in its original meaning also meant that the kinsman would recover sold or forfeited inheritance. He was the chief defender not only of the person but also of the possessions of the one over whom he was a protector. This was a part of the Mosaic Code.

The loss of Paradise was for man a tragedy. Sin made him forfeit his spiritual inheritance; it disfranchised him of his heavenly citizenship; it robbed him of his nobility; it left him a miserable pauper. But Christ as our Redeemer has recovered our lost estate for us if we will accept His act of redemption. He is the Elder Brother, our great Kinsman, who undertook to win back for us that which we had lost.

This text and title is also animated with three vital concepts of our faith—immortality, resurrection, and the return of Jesus Christ. It bespeaks our ultimate redemption by our immortal and invincible Kinsman.

O Christ, my Kinsman, thank You for redeeming my soul from the clutches of Satan and the consequences of sin. I accept and rejoice in this glorious liberty purchased at such tremendous cost.

Portrait 4

Lily of the Valley

I am . . . the lily of the valleys.

Song of Solomon 2:1

From this allegorical book of the Bible, we have this title ascribed to and associated with Christ through the centuries. This verse also gives us the companion title, "Rose of Sharon."

It is suggested that the lily was the scarlet martagon or the white amaryllis. The rose of Sharon was probably the common and abundant meadow-saffron, crocus, or narcissus.

In what ways are these flowers suggestive of Christ in His character and mission?

First of all they speak of His humility. This verse, according to exegetes, could well read, "I am but a wild flower in the plain, a lowly lily of the valleys." Like these lowly flowers of the field ready to be trodden under the foot of man and crushed, Christ humbled Himself and exposed Himself to the bestiality and brutality of men.

The white amaryllis is only three inches from the ground and has a drooping head. It is emblematic of humility and the One who said, ". . .learn of me; for I am meek and lowly in heart."

Secondly, these titles speak of the beauty of Christ. Jesus spoke of the lilies of the field as adorned with a beauty to which all the glory of Solomon could not be compared. The wild flowers of Palestine were very beautiful. What was more beautiful than the life of Jesus Christ? It was beautiful in purity, in holiness, in love and compassion, in holy power, in radiant joy and goodness. The late Albert Orsborn's words express the heart's longing to partake of that beauty:

> Let the beauty of Jesus be seen in me,
> All His wonderful passion and purity;
> Oh, Thou Spirit divine, All my nature refine,
> Till the beauty of Jesus be seen in me.

Thirdly, the titles are suggestive of the fragrance that was diffused from His life. The white amaryllis was especially sweet-scented.

In a valley of Rumania, roses are grown for the Vienna market in great profusion and with much distillation of fragrance. We are told that if you were to visit that valley at the time of the rose crop, wherever you would go the rest of the day, the fragrance you would carry with you would betray where you had been.

There is a beautiful parable given us by the Persian poet and moralist, Saadi. The poet was given a bit of ordinary clay. The clay was so redolent with sweet perfume that its fragrance filled all the room.

"What are you, musk or ambergris?" he questioned.
"I am neither," it answered. "I am just a bit of common clay."
"From where then do you have this rare perfume?" the poet asked.
"I have companied all the summer with the rose," it replied.

We are just bits of the common clay of humanity. But if we company with the One who is the Rose of Sharon and the Lily of the Valley, something of the fragrance of His life will pass into ours. Then we will be a freshening and a sweetening influence to the world around us.

Jesus, Thou Rose of Sharon and Lily of the Valley, bloom in all Thy beauty in the garden of my heart.

Portrait 5

Wonderful Counselor

> . . . and his name shall be called Wonderful, Counselor.
> Isaiah 9:6

The traditional King James Version of the Bible separates the above as two titles, but more recent Bible scholars regard the comma between them as an error. Modern translations such as the Revised Standard Version and the Amplified New Testament tend to render this title as "Wonderful Counselor."

Isaiah has given us, in this magnificent verse, a constellation of titles. Its lofty appellations declare the superlative qualities of the Messianic King. The first title emphasizes His wisdom.

We cannot deny our need for wise counsel and our reliance upon divine guidance. Life is often perplexing, bewildering, complex, problematic, disconcerting. We have an inescapable need for the Divine Counselor.

A counselor is one who advises, instructs, and guides in directing the judgment and conduct of another. He is involved in the intimacies of life, directing it through its crises and critical periods. Counselors become custodians of the crises of life. It is a staggering responsibility. It is a sacred responsibility. What are the essential qualifications of a counselor?

A counselor needs to be *close,* accessible. Jesus Christ is as close as the whisper of a prayer. He is always available, never away or too busy. He will ever attend to our prayer and help us in our need.

The *confidential* aspect of counseling is inherent in Christ's counseling to His followers. To Him, we can take the most intimate matters of the heart.

He is *compassionate*—tender, loving, concerned for us. To Him we are not a case, but a child; not a problem person, but a person with a problem and potential.

He is *cognizant* of us and our needs and He knows what is best for us. A counselor must have a good knowledge of the person to be counseled. Some counselors fail because they never achieve a thorough understanding of the person. It is difficult indeed to penetrate the subtleties of human emotions, motivation, and the makeup of our subconscious which dictates so much of our conscious life. The inspired chronicler writes: ". . . he knew all men, And needed not that any should testify of man: for he knew what was in man" (John 2:24,25). Jesus Christ knows and understands us better than we know ourselves. He is the specialist of the human heart.

As a counselor He is *capable.* He has all the resources of power and help to put at our disposal. He is omniscient. He is wisdom incarnate. He is inerrant in His counsel to us. He will always guide our steps aright.

Another essential qualification of a counselor is that he be able to *communicate* and enable the person to discover the resources needed for his situation. We can communicate to Christ in prayer. How does He communicate to us? Is not prayer a dialogue rather than a monologue? If we exercise the discipline of silence and stillness, does not Christ speak to us through inward promptings, the engenderings of convictions, the sensitizing of conscience? Does He not also speak to us through the gentle stirrings of His Spirit? And has He not left for us His *counselor's manual* for the human heart in the communication of His Word?

Indeed Christ is the Counselor par excellence. He is the Wonderful Counselor.

> O Christ, Wonderful Counselor, I would yield my foolishness to Thy wisdom, my perplexity to Thy guidance, my darkness to Thy light, my future to Thy prescience, my life to Thy way and will.

Portrait 6

The Mighty God

> . . . and his name shall be called . . . The mighty God.
>
> Isaiah 9:6

Many have tried to escape the force of this declaration. However, Scripture, history, and human experience corroborate its sacred and sublime truth.

In St. John's prologue to his Gospel, he gives us a breathtaking opening statement that declares three transcendent truths about Jesus Christ:

1. He was eternally existent—"In the beginning was the Word."
2. He had fellowship with God—"and the Word was with God."
3. He was God—"and the Word was God."

In that same prologue we read, "All things were made by him and without him was not any thing made that was made" (John 1:3). The same truth is reaffirmed in the Pauline text of Colossians 1:16. Jesus is declared to have been an agent of creation. Even before He came to earth, His hands tumbled solar systems and galaxies into space. He set the stars on their courses. He kindled the fires of the sun. He scooped out the giant beds of our mighty oceans.

> His holy fingers formed the bough
>   Where grew the thorns that crowned His brow,
> The nails that pierced the hands were mined
>   In secret places He designed.
>
> He made the forests whence there sprung
>   The tree on which His holy body hung,
> He died upon a cross of wood
>   Yet made the hill upon which it stood.
>
> The sun which hid from Him its face
>   By His decree was poised in space.
> The sky which darkened o'er His head
>   By Him above the earth was spread.
>
> F.W. PITT

He was the Mighty God in His preincarnate glory and splendor. He was mighty in His birth when time was invaded by eternity and split in two. He was mighty in His ministry and His incomparable miracles. He was mighty in His teachings, putting the imperishable truths of the Kingdom into word forms so indestructible that man could never forget them. He was mighty in His death as He rescued us from the hell we deserve and made us heirs to the heaven we forfeited. He was mighty in His Resurrection as He arose, the Mighty Conqueror, over man's last enemy. He will be mighty as He comes again in His matchless and transcendent glory.

> O Mighty God who holds the world in Your power, thank You for holding my frail life in Your mighty hands.

Portrait 7

The Everlasting Father

> . . . and his name shall be called . . . The everlasting Father.
> Isaiah 9:6

We usually associate the name of Father with the first Person of the Godhead, but here the title belongs to Christ. However the original text does not denote *father* in the usual association we have with that word. It means in this verse *author* or *possessor*. A more exact rendering of this verse would be "the Father of Eternity" as it is rendered by the American Standard Version and the Amplified Old Testament. Thus, this verse speaks of Christ as the Eternal One and as the One who holds eternity in His possession. Vast, unfathomable eternity is His.

One of the most intriguing exercises for the imagination is to consider the eternity of Jesus. It staggers the mind. Jesus always was; He had no beginning. As God, He is the great First Cause of all things. If we could turn back the time clock and look down the dim corridor of the ages, we would find Jesus with the Father at the beginning. He was there when the planets and the universe were created. He antedates the eons of time geologists tell us were involved in the creation of our planet. He is the unbeginning One.

He is also the Contemporary of every age. Recall His last words to His disciples. With His heavenly throne in view, the harps of glory sounding in His ears, He reassures His pilgrim church with the music of these precious words, ". . . Lo, I am with you alway, even unto the end of the world" (Matthew 28:20).

People ask, "Who *were* Buddha and Napoleon?" But always, "Who IS Jesus Christ?"

Not only is Jesus Lord of the past and the present, but, as the possessor of eternity, He holds the future in His hands. Jesus the timeless, holds all time in His hands. We may not know what the future holds, but we know who holds the future.

Because Jesus Christ is eternal and He has made us joint heirs with Him, we shall share eternity with Him. The short day of our earthly life is only a prelude and a brief preparation for the higher life that is beyond. Our life is larger and longer than we dream. Eternal forces ripple in our blood, voices from afar call us to an eternal destiny.

He who is the Father of eternity links us with our Heavenly Father so that we will share the bliss of eternal ages with Him.

Eternal Christ, help me to so pass through things temporal that I shall not forfeit the things that are eternal.

Portrait 8

The Prince of Peace

> ... and his name shall be called ... the Prince of Peace.
>
> Isaiah 9:6

Peace often seems to be the most sought for and, at the same time, the most elusive treasure. The great cry of the world is for peace. The diligent and devoted effort of so many world leaders and diplomats is on behalf of peace. Yet history seems to mock their effort and confirm the futility of man's search for peace. A famous French historian estimated that there had been 3,130 years of war in contrast to 227 years of peace from the fifteenth century before Christ to his own day. The world had seen thirteen years of war for every year of peace.

Today nuclear destruction threatens civilization as cities and nations stand only by sufferance and often seem headed on a collision course with annihilation. In the next deadly game of war, the score will be kept in units of a million corpses.

This is not only the era of the split atom but of the split personality as well. Man is beset by neuroses and psychoses that undermine his peace from within. The fears of man are so many and varied that psychologists have charted them all the way from *a* to *z*: acrophobia, fear of heights, to zoophobia, fear of animals. People cannot sleep. Americans are the champion insomniacs, consuming over three billion pills a year. The classic words of Henry Thoreau seem more apposite to our age than to his time, "The mass of men lead lives of quiet desperation."

The heart of the problem is the problem of the heart. Peace is not so much an external climate as it is an inward experience. It gives inner equilibrium to the life amidst the disquietude without. As the Prince of Peace, Jesus imparts His peace that applies to three primary relationships.

First of all, He enables us to have peace *with God* by His work of reconciliation. Sin separated and estranged man from God. The cross of Calvary was a great bridge across the impassable chasm of sin. It led the way from man's fallen condition back to his holy Creator. Augustine once wrote:

> Thou hast made us for Thyself, and the heart of man is restless until it finds its rest in Thee.

Secondly, Jesus enables us to have peace *within ourselves*. He resolves the inner conflicts, cross purposes, and tensions which act as bandits robbing us of serenity. He quells the civil war within the heart, between the carnal and the spiritual nature, by the power and work of the Holy Spirit.

When we are at peace with God and with ourselves, then we will be at peace in the third area of relationship—with others. Having truly discovered the Fatherhood of God we will learn to practice the brotherhood of man. When the vertical relationship is right then the horizontal relationship will take on its proper perspective.

Thou Prince of Peace, so attune my heart that there will be no disharmony of desire, no discord of selfishness. Help me by Thy atonement to have attunement within my own heart and in my relationships.

Portrait 9

Rod and Branch

And there shall come forth a rod out of the stem of Jesse, and a Branch shall grow out of his roots.

Isaiah 11:1

Jesse was a father of kings. David, Solomon, Hezekiah, and Josiah came from his lineage, but now that kingly line was as a truncated tree. Isaiah is prophesying that from that stump will grow a Stem and a Branch that shall become greater than all that grew before it.

God would keep alive the roots of the family tree of Jesse as revealed in the intriguing genealogies of Matthew and Luke.

This verse reveals Christ's inseparable link with history. History is subject to God's sovereignty. Christ's birth in Bethlehem (as prophesied centuries before by Micah) was no geographical happenstance. His birth at the most fortuitous period was no historical coincidence. For it was then that communication of the Gospel would be most expeditious via the Roman highways and the Greek language. His birth of the lineage of Jesse was no genealogical accident. *"There shall come forth . . . ."* History has certain predictable elements as it falls under the sovereignty of God. There are junctures at which God intervenes. History is His story.

In the cataclysmic events of our day, it is greatly reassuring that God overrules history. Those who today would publish the obituary of God would do well to ponder the divine thread that is interwoven with the ages. It has not been severed in this so-called postmodern world. God is still on the throne.

Not only does this title suggest Christ's link with history in His invincible sovereignty over its course, but it would remind us of His superiority over earth's monarchs. The other kings of David's line have been buried in the sands of time. Their empires have vanished. Their gold tarnished and their influence spent its little day. All other rulers pale into insignificance next to His transcendent splendor. His is an unapproachable glory, an unexampled sublimity, an ineffable majesty.

O Christ, Thou center and sovereign of history, rule over my life, my will, my future.

Portrait 10

Man of Sorrows

He is despised and rejected of men; a man of sorrows, and acquainted with grief. . . .

Isaiah 53:3

This title and the portrait of the Master it gives to us is so indelibly etched in the pages of the New Testament that it immediately stands out as one of the cardinal titles of Christ. Some notable men are men of wealth, some are men of fame, some are men of pleasure, but Christ was a Man of Sorrows. He was the Prince of martyrs, the Lord of anguish, the King of suffering. Some of His closest followers might forsake Him, but His sorrows were always with Him.

The last week of Christ's earthly life, with its record of deep sorrow, looms most prominently in the Gospels. One-third of Matthew, one-third of Mark, one-fourth of Luke, and one-half of John's Gospel is devoted to the last week of the life of Jesus. This is in striking contrast to the few pages of biography covering the death of other men of history. An example is a biography of Abraham Lincoln with only twenty-five out of its five thousand pages relating the dramatic account of the assassination and death. The amount of space in the Gospels devoted to Christ's suffering and death is so disproportionate as to underscore the paramount value of that period in His life and ministry.

I am amazed that God loved me enough to be born as a man. I stand in even greater awe that He loved me enough to suffer earth's deepest agony and most humiliating death. It is too deep for me to plumb its mystery and majesty. Deity becoming incarnate is in itself a marvel of the ages. That Incarnate Deity should be so predominantly characterized by sorrow makes us aware that, as we think on this title, we are entering into the Holy of Holies in the santuary of Christ's life. We are standing before one of the most sublime and sacred truths of eternity.

The sorrows and anguish of Jesus defy description or definition. The depths of His devotion transcend our finite comprehension. His love was wounded in betrayal and denial by those of His most intimate circle. He was burdened with the weight of the awesome responsibility for the redemption of the whole world. His soul suffered the awful pressure of imputed condemnation for man's transgressions. His body felt keenly the torture and excruciating pain of the cross. He had to endure ignominy, mockery of His love, dying thirst, shame, guilt, and the death of the cross. There was utter dereliction and loneliness in Christ's suffering at Calvary. Oh, to what fathomless depths God descended to rescue a dying world!

Some years ago when we were having family devotions, one of our little girls was quite struck by the fact that Jesus suffered so much on Calvary. Quite unaware of the theological profundity of her question, she asked in deep sincerity, "But if Jesus was God, why did He have to die?" As we contemplate the unexampled sorrows and sufferings of Christ, we cannot help but to cry out, "Why? Why?" Isaiah answers this question for us in immortal words:

> Surely he has borne our griefs
>   and carried our sorrows;
> yet we esteemed him stricken,
>   smitten by God, and afflicted.
>
> But he was wounded for our transgressions,
>   he was bruised for our iniquities;
> upon him was the chastisement that made us whole,
>   and with his stripes we are healed.
>
> All we like sheep have gone astray;
>   we have turned every one to his own way;
> and the Lord had laid on him
>   the iniquity of us all.
>
> Isaiah 53:4–6 RSV

The nails that tore through His sacred hands and feet were our sins. The thorns that pierced His brow and marred His visage were our sins. The scourge that lacerated the flesh of His back to ribbons was our sin. The wagging heads that mocked Him and the tongues that vilified Him were our sins.

"He was wounded for our transgressions." As the Man of Sorrows He took upon Himself our burden and penalty of sin. He bore it for us. He carried our sorrow. He suffered our condemnation. He endured our agony. He died our death.

O Man of Sorrows, thank You for Your sufferings on my behalf. Save me from seeking comfort in place of the cross, security in place of sacrifice. Give me grace and strength to tread the winepress with You.

Portrait II

Messiah

Know therefore and understand, that from the going forth of the commandment to restore and to build Jerusalem unto the Messiah the Prince shall be seven weeks, and threescore and two weeks. . . . And after threescore and two weeks shall Messiah be cut off. . . .

Daniel 9:25,26

Bible characters are portrayed with brutal candor, "warts and all." However, Daniel is one of the very few in the Bible whose life is presented without any faults. For over seventy years, he served God with steadfast devotion in a foreign land and as a member of a pagan court. His character was irreproachable throughout his long and fruitful life. The secret of his high moral excellence was his prayer life. Daniel was above all else a man of prayer.

In this ninth chapter, there is recorded his eloquent and lofty prayer of intercession. Now over eighty years of age, he is an elder statesman, a vice-president in the palace of one of the world's great empires. His mind and heart are not on the luxuries of the palace but on the plight of his people. He thought of their exile and the destitution of their city and temple. Thus he is moved to this remarkable prayer that was accompanied by a study of the writings of Jeremiah, and with fasting and sackcloth. He poured out his soul in earnest intercession for his people and their calamity.

It was a very special prayer. God gave him a very special answer.

God's answer through the angel Gabriel far exceeded Daniel's petition. He prayed for the holy city and its temple and people, but God would send One whose blessings and glory would extend far beyond the bounds of Jerusalem. How often His answers and provisions exceed our askings. In answer to his prayer, God vouchsafes to Daniel a revelation of the coming Messiah. Thus this sacred title is born. It would be the name that would express men's longing and expectation through those silent years of the intertestament period.

Messiah means *the Anointed One.* Its Greek equivalent is *Christ.*

In Old Testament times, there were three offices that involved an anointing with holy oil. Prophets, priests, and kings were thus installed in their offices. Jesus, as the anointed of God, is all three to His followers. He is our Prophet, Priest, and King. The anointing oil has become a symbol of the Holy Spirit, thus making this title further emblematic.

This revelation of the Messiah pertained not only to His *coming* but also to His *chronology.* Not only was there revealed the person of the Messiah but also the period of the Messiah. It is generally accepted that each week represents seven years so that the "seventy weeks" would be 490 years. This period of seventy weeks reckoned "from the going forth of the commandment to restore and to build Jerusalem." In 457 B.C. King Artaxerxes commissioned Ezra to rebuild Jerusalem. The sixty-nine prophetic weeks of v.25 equals 483 years, which from the date of 457 B.C. brings us to A.D. 26, about the time Jesus is believed to have been baptized. This is representative of His being set apart for the sacrifice for man's sin. The final or seventieth prophetic week (seven years) was the period in which the Gospel was extended to the Gentile world. Between the sixty-ninth and seventieth prophetic weeks, the Messiah would be "cut off."

In this extraordinary revelation to Daniel, not only did God reveal the coming and the chronology of the Messiah but also the *course of events* associated with His coming. These are delineated in verses 24–27 and include:

1. ". . . To finish the transgression, and to make an end of sins . . .
2. "To make reconciliation for iniquity . . .
3. "To bring in everlasting righteousness . . .
4. "To seal up the vision and prophecy." All Messianic prophecies would have had their fulfillment in Christ.
5. "To anoint the most Holy," or literally "Holy of holies." Christ as the new "Holy of holies" would replace the former tabernacle and temple mentioned in the prayer of Daniel.
6. The Messiah would be "cut off"—a reference to His violent death.
7. Jerusalem would be destroyed by a great overflowing of war—a reference to its destruction in A.D. 70.
8. "And shall confirm the covenant with many . . .
9. "He shall cause the sacrifice . . . to cease." All sacrifices were but types and foreshadowings of His great offering. His death would end the period of legal sacrifices.

O Christ, satisfy the deepest longings and expectations of my heart and fulfill Thy holy purpose in my life.

Portrait 12

King

Rejoice greatly, O daughter of Zion; shout, O daughter of Jerusalem: behold, thy King cometh unto thee: he is just, and having salvation; lowly, and riding upon an ass, and upon a colt the foal of an ass.

Zechariah 9:9

This prophecy is inseparably linked with the Triumphal Entry. The Gospel writer states that the Triumphal Entry was in fulfillment of this very prophecy (Matthew 21:4,5).

Zechariah enjoins the people to shout, for His coming would be an epochal event that would merit their most enthusiastic and exuberant response. In our text and its context, some salient features of His kingdom are given.

He would usher in a *kingdom of joy.* "Rejoice greatly" was the injunction to the people. He is the King who would announce, "I am come that they might have life, and that they might have it more abundantly" (John 10:10). Dr. Ramsey, Archbishop of Canterbury, sharing in a Salvation Army Centennial service with Her Majesty Queen Elizabeth, paid Salvationists an unforgettable tribute: "I don't think I've ever seen a gloomy member of The Salvation Army." This statement can of course be said of all true Christians. Christ puts a spring in the step, a smile on the countenance, a radiance in the life. He is the King of Joy.

His would also be a kingdom of justice. So many of earth's kingdoms are ruled by injustice marked by graft, crime, dishonesty, expediency, inequities. But Christ's kingdom will be characterized by justice. It is assured by His character and power—"He is just." He is the King of Justice.

"And having salvation" speaks of the deliverance He will bring His people from the serfdom of sin. He will make His people free. He will liberate them from their spiritual disfranchisement. ". . . By the blood of thy covenant I have sent forth thy prisoners out of the pit" (Zechariah 9:11). Sin has often been made analogous to a pit. The pits of that day were miry at the bottom. The only opening was at the top through which the prisoner was thrown into the pit. Escape was impossible, but Christ gives hope. He came to bring salvation from the deep and inescapable pit of sin—"by the blood of [His] covenant." He is the King of Salvation.

Our text also speaks of Him as a "lowly" King. He was not dependent on the props of earthly monarchs. He would not come with the pageantry and pomp of earth's transient kings. He would not mount a war horse, but at His procession, would ride on an animal that was the symbol of quietness. His coming would be accompanied by palm branches rather than spears. Not the shouts of soldiers but the songs of children and the lilting "hosannas" would be the music of His coming.

His would also be a kingdom of peace—"he shall speak peace" (v. 10). Some kings have been noted for their great battles and victories, or defeats. But others have been more renowned for their reigns of peace. Man through history has not been able to learn the lesson of peace. He is inclined to war which is collective madness. But Christ is the King of Peace.

Finally, the prophet declares the universality of His kingdom, "His dominion shall be from sea even to sea" (v. 10). Not only will it be without geographical boundaries, but also without time or race barriers. All people of all places of all times who have acknowledged His reign over life shall be citizens of His great kingdom. He is the King of the universe.

Thou Mighty King of the universe, rule every motive, thought, and deed of my life. May my fidelity and service help to usher in Thy kingdom of peace.

Portrait 13

Messenger of the Covenant

Behold . . . the Lord, whom ye seek, shall suddenly come to his temple, even the messenger of the covenant, whom ye delight in: behold, he shall come, saith the Lord of hosts.

Malachi 3:1

There is an inspiring and progressive history of the covenant in the Bible. There was the Noachian Covenant (Genesis 9:11), when God promised the preservation of mankind and confirmed it with the token of the "bow in the cloud." The Abrahamic Covenant (Genesis 15:18) was entered into with impressive and symbolic ceremony which gave promise of the inheritance of the Jewish nation. Then, as Israel came to age as a people, God entered into the Sinaitic Covenant (Exodus 34:10) which established His relationship with them as a nation. David's final words speak of the "everlasting covenant" (2 Samuel 23:5) God entered into with him.

There are several essential characteristics of the biblical covenant:

1. It was a solemn and sacred agreement between God and man.
2. God was the initiator. The finite cannot initiate agreement with the infinite.
3. Man was always the benefactor. The biblical covenants would always foretoken some great blessing to man from God.

4. The covenant related to collective bodies. It was not merely with the individual but with his family and posterity. Noah was the representative of mankind. The covenant with Abraham was to his seed forever. Moses was the representative of the Jewish nation. The covenant with David applied to all the lineage of the great king.

In the latter period of the Old Testament, there unfolded the concept of the new covenant God would establish with man. Jeremiah declared God would make a "new covenant" (Jeremiah 31:31). It would be a spiritual covenant and would be universal in its inclusion of all people. In the New Testament, we read, ". . . Jesus has become the Guarantee of a better (stronger) agreement—a more excellent and more advantageous covenant" (Hebrews 7:22 AMPLIFIED NEW TESTAMENT). He is also called the "mediator of a better covenant" (Hebrews 8:6).

The word *testament* is equivalent to *covenant*. Thus the two major divisions of the Bible could rightly be called "The Old and the New Covenant."

This progressive covenant relationship has its ultimate unfolding in Jesus Christ. His redemption was the new covenant between God and man.

Malachi prophesies that the Lord will come as the Messenger of the Covenant. He will inaugurate, announce, and implement the new covenant with mankind. That God should enter into covenant with man is a gracious act of condescension. To contemplate its marvel staggers the mind, but it captivates the heart.

"He shall come, saith the Lord." With those words the voice of prophecy was silenced for over four centuries. But man had this great promise. Thank God, He keeps His promises. The Messenger of the Covenant did come and man entered into a new and living way in relationship with God.

O Christ, thank You for entering into covenant with me by Your sacrifice on Calvary. Help me not only to accept its gracious benefits but also to carry out its solemn responsibilities.

Portrait 14

Sun of Righteousness

But unto you who revere and worshipfully fear My name shall the Sun of righteousness arise with healing in His wings and His beams, and you shall go forth and gambol like calves released from the stall and leap for joy.

Malachi 4:2 AMPLIFIED NEW TESTAMENT

What the sun is to the earth, Christ is to the soul. Christians have aptly been called heliotropes. These are plants (such as the sunflower) that turn their faces toward the sun. Their leaves hang as in sadness when the sun is withdrawn. So the Christian is one who has turned toward the Sun of Righteousness and receives from Him life and beauty.

The sun is our source of *light.* Without its illumination, our earth would be a dark and sterile planet. Christ is our source of spiritual light. He dispels darkness and diffuses His radiant light throughout the world and in the heart of man.

The sun is also a source of *life.* In the fall in our part of the world, there takes place a death of nature. Plants, flowers, and grass fade and die as the winter months approach. But then when springtime comes around again, a miracle takes place. There is a resurrection, a rejuvenation. Tender shoots push their way through the soil. Protoplasm is activated in every tree and begins the manufacture of new leaves, buds, and blossoms. There is an inexorable energy received from the sun which produces this new life. So is there a spiritual life that is dormant within each person. All it needs is to bask in the glow of the Sun of Righteousness to be resurrected to its potential of life and growth.

The sun is also a source of *beauty*. Brightness and color come from the benign rays of the sun. The sun reveals the expansive beauty of the blue sky, the restful green of the trees and verdant meadows, the kaleidoscopic beauty of a garden. The Sun of Righteousness would adorn a life with the rich hues of His grace and make it beautiful. He will beautify the character, the personality, the relationships, and all of life.

The sun is also the *center* of our solar system, our sphere of life. At one time the universe was considered to have been geocentric—centering in the earth with everything else revolving around our planet. This was the Ptolemaic system and under that concept none of the sums would come out right. But when Copernicus discovered the heliocentric principle, the sun as the center of our universe with everything revolving around it, then science made sense. Everything added up to an intelligent sum. This is analogous to our spiritual life. When life becomes egocentric, self-centered, then it is inane and futile. It is ec entric, off center. But when we have the Sun of Righteousness as the center of our life, then it takes on purpose and meaning. It comes out right.

Our text also states that the Sun of Righteousness will have "healing in His wings." Sin brought death and destruction for the soul and body, but Christ in His salvation brings *healing* for the disease of sin. His benignant rays will dispel the germ of sin and bring health to the soul.

The final thought of our text is that the delivered soul will be like a calf that has been confined to the stall and is suddenly freed. It gambols and cavorts and skips and leaps. So there is an *exuberance of life* imparted by the Sun of Righteousness.

The first promise made to Adam was as a feeble spark. But here, in the last book of prophecy, that spark has through the centuries become enlarged until now it has become the Sun of Righteousness that will bring illumination to the whole world.

Thou Sun of Righteousness, illumine all my being with Thy beneficent radiance so that my life will be aglow with Thy light and beauty.

II
The Advent

Names and Titles Associated With the Advent of Jesus Christ

- **15** Son of David
- **16** Jesus
- **17** Emmanuel
- **18** Horn of Salvation

Portrait 15

Son of David

The book of the generation of Jesus Christ, the son of David. . . .
Matthew 1:1

To us, today, this title may not seem too significant. However, the first question put forward in Christ's day about an alleged Messiah would be: "Is he of the house of David?" Any claimant to the title of Messiah would have to pass this genealogical muster. Every devout Jew knew that God had promised, through His prophets, that the Messiah would come from the lineage of David. This genealogical table was necessary to certify Christ's Messiahship.

Our text reveals that the tapestry of history is woven with threads from the looms of God. Matthew, with his gift for detail, has arranged His genealogical table into three divisions of fourteen generations each. The first period takes us from Abraham to David, from the patriarchs and judges to the period of the monarchy. The second period is from David to the exile and represents both the flowering and the fading of the kingdom. The final period is that of the exile and the postexilic period, a time when Israel could have passed into oblivion except for divine providence. It is remarkable that all through these periods, some extremely critical, God preserved the seed of Abraham and David from which would come Christ. History is His story.

It is intriguing to study the names of the genealogy. There are four women, some of them with scandalous and unsavory backgrounds. Ruth represents blood other than that of Jewish exclusiveness. Some of the names are nondescript and represent anything but luminaries on the horizon of history. The last ten names are unrecorded in the Old Testament, but how wonderfully God uses the weak things, the seemingly insignificant, to bring about His purpose. Each one of the names listed was a vital link in God's chain of history.

This title also links Jesus with humanity. He was born of earthly parentage. Although He was God, He became a man. He was the Ancient of Days, yet He was born at a point in time. He created worlds and companied with celestial beings, yet He came to live in a family setting upon earth.

This title, and its context, also speaks of the royalty of Jesus Christ. There is an accent in this listing of names on the royal family of Israel. Christ was a descendent of the royal line of David and Israel's kings. However, He transcended all the royalty that was represented in this title. The effulgent glory of His regal splendor pales into insignificance the smoking flax of earth's kings. He brought a glory and a grandeur to the throne of David that will be undimmed and undiminished throughout eternal ages. Time is but His courier and eternity His habitation in contrast to the ephemeral reigns of earth's monarchs.

He who was the Son of God became the Son of David, that we might be of His spiritual lineage and be forever adopted as sons of God.

O Christ of infinite love, I thank You for making it possible for me to be born into the great family of our Heavenly Father. Enable me to ever be His faithful and loving child.

Portrait 16

Jesus

> *... thou shalt call his name JESUS: for he shall save his people from their sins.*
>
> Matthew 1:21

Our verse starts with a *declaration,* "thou shalt call." The name *Jesus* was the name God Himself chose. God sent His own messenger from the heavenly courts and through the celestial corridors to announce what His name should be.

Then there is the *designation,* "Jesus." It is the name by which we know Him best. It is His earthly name. Other names and titles were ascribed to Him in special ways and for a specific purpose, but this is His primary name. In the Gospels, He is called by this name over five hundred times.

Of all the names and titles this is the one that has been most endearing to His followers. The contents of a hymnbook add eloquent testimony of that fact: John Newton's immortal words, "How sweet the name of Jesus sounds"; Charles Wesley rhapsodized, "Jesus! the Name high over all"; Edward Perronet exalts this name with "All hail the power of Jesus' Name!"; Bernard leads us to devotional depths with his, "Jesus! the very thought of Thee"; Baxter earnestly enjoins, "Take the Name of Jesus with you"; Frederick Whitfield exclaims, "There is a name I love to hear"; and Will Brand indites, "There is beauty in the name of Jesus."

Our text gives not only the declaration and the designation of this name but also its *denotation*—"He shall save His people from their sins." It is the name that denotes the great purpose of His life. Above all else He came to be our Saviour. Imagine knowing Tennyson, but not as a poet; Shakespeare, but not as a litterateur; Socrates, but not as a philosopher! Unless we know Jesus as Saviour, we miss the predominant message and mission of His life.

The names *Jesus* and *Joshua* are the same. *Joshua* is the Hebrew equivalent of the Greek *Jesus.* Many Bible scholars consider Joshua to have been a prototype of Christ. The names are the same with the same denotation. There are striking points of correspondency between the type and the prototype. Joshua led the Israelites from the wilderness into the Promised Land. Jesus as Saviour brings us from the wilderness of sin into our spiritual Promised Land. Joshua led his people to conquests over their enemies with their walled cities and tall giants. So Jesus leads us to conquest over the enemies of our soul. He enables us to fight victoriously against life's difficult obstacles and its giants of temptation, trial, and testing. As our Joshua, He leads us to the inheritance God has for us—a land spiritually "flowing with milk and honey."

Jesus, of course, far transcended Joshua's work of salvation among the people. Joshua's deliverance foreshadowed and prefigured the One who would give ultimate fulfillment to this great name. "Neither is there salvation in any other: for there is none other name under heaven given among men, whereby we must be saved" (Acts 4:12).

Jesus, Thou art a Mighty Saviour. I have come to You for there is no one else to whom I can go for my salvation and security.

Portrait 17

Emmanuel

Behold, a virgin shall be with child, and shall bring forth a son, and they shall call his name Emmanuel, which being interpreted is, God with us.

Matthew 1:23

God had this name written three times in His Word: Isaiah 7:14; 8:8; and in our text. In the Gospel account, the angel in his announcement to Joseph is quoting the prophet Isaiah. It was elected to reserve this title for this portion of our study rather than to have included it in the Old Testament because of its direct relation to the Advent.

Christ alone was great enough to be called Emmanuel. No one else could fill its glowing meaning—*God with us.*

John gives us a graphic portrait of Christ among us when he wrote that He "... became flesh (human, incarnate), and tabernacled—fixed His tent of flesh, lived awhile—among us; and we [actually] saw His glory" (John 1:14 AMPLIFIED NEW TESTAMENT). This thought of God fixing His tent of flesh and living among us is a stupendous one. It is almost inconceivable. It staggers the imagination. Yet that is precisely what happened with the Incarnation.

The miracle and the marvel of *Emmanuel*—God with us—defies description. The hands of God that had tumbled solar systems into space became the small chubby hands of an infant. The feet of God that had roamed through fiery planets became the infant feet of a baby. Jesus was the heart of God wrapped in human flesh. He was

God in the garb of humanity. He was God walking the earth in sandals.

A young child looked at a picture of her absent father and longingly said, "I wish Father would step out of that picture." For centuries, men had a yearning for God to step out of the picture—to become more real, more tangible to man. Men wanted to know God better, what He was like, and to commune with Him. At Bethlehem, God became flesh—became real, understandable to men. Jesus was God's authentic self-disclosure.

What a reassuring thought it is that He is still *Emmanuel* to His followers. He is still *God with us.* He has promised, "Lo, I am with you alway, even unto the end of the world" (Matthew 28:20). We follow the One who said, "I will never leave thee, nor forsake thee" (Hebrew 13:5). He is always the contemporary Christ. He is superior to all life's vicissitudes, surviving death itself. He will walk with us through its valley into the house of the Lord where we shall dwell with Him forever.

O Christ, my Emmanuel, abide with me all through life. Thus enriched by Thy fellowship, strengthened by Thy presence, and led by Thy guidance, I shall adequately walk life's path.

Portrait 18

Horn of Salvation

And hath raised up an horn of salvation for us. . . .

Luke 1:69

In Luke's account of the Advent are several songlike passages. They could be called hymns, each one flowing in style and having its own inherent message. Some churches today still incorporate words from these hymns in their liturgy. There was the Annunciation (Luke 1:28–37) by the angel Gabriel who was entrusted with the most superlative message ever sent from heaven to earth. Mary's song of praise (Luke 1:46–55) was expressed in the exultant words of her *Magnificat*. There is also bequeathed to us the *Benedictus* (Luke 1:68–79) by Zacharias, the *Nunc dimittis* (Luke 2:25–35) by Simeon, and the lovely canticle by Elizabeth (Luke 1:42). And on that night of nights the heavens rang out with the *Gloria in Excelsis* by the herald angels.

A newspaper cartoon during the Christmas season pictured a father and mother with their small children looking at a store window with its decoration and display of merchandise. In the center of the window is a large sign, "Let's make this the best Christmas ever." The father gives the punch line with, "How are they ever going to top the FIRST one?" May our recurring attention to the Christmas story each year not dull us to the wonder of that first Christmas when time was invaded by eternity with a beachhead established on Bethlehem's shore. Those who had a part in that great drama of the ages and have given us their inspired utterances would remind us again of the miracle of Christ coming to earth. The title under consideration comes to

53

us from the *Benedictus* of Zacharias.

"Horn of Salvation" is a title with a latitude of interpretations. In the metaphorical title of this verse, it primarily denotes strength and power. Goodspeed renders this title "A Mighty Saviour." Horns grew on the male animal and the bull was the strongest of the herd. It would fight off the herd's enemies by lowering its head and charging fiercely, and woe to whatever might find itself on the end of its horn. He was the protector of the herd from its deadly predators. Thus, Christ as the Horn of Salvation, is our great Protector. He defends us against the deadly foes of the soul. We are delivered by His mighty salvation.

In Bible days, the horn was also a drinking vessel. A small horn of an animal would often be cut in such a way as to make a very useful type of drinking cup. From Christ, we receive and drink of the living water which satisfies the deepest thirsts of our lives.

The horn was also a musical instrument. The ram's horn was quite long and used as a trumpet. We are reminded that Christ replaces the discord of a life with His harmony. His presence and power can make life like a symphony with all its parts—emotions, thoughts, experiences, deeds, affections—contributing to a harmonious blending of the whole.

Finally, there were the horns of the altar. The horns were the corners and the most sacred part of the altar. There a fugitive could take hold and be protected from his pursuer. Nearby would be the sacred colors of gold and blue, purple and scarlet, the sweet-smelling incense, the bells and pomegranates, the vestments and other trappings. But none of these could avail for the person in deadly distress. The horns alone offered refuge. On the crude altar of the cross, Jesus made the great sacrifice so that we might take hold of Him and find refuge for our souls.

O Mighty Christ, turn my weakness into power.

III
The Person

The I Ams or Self-Ascribed Titles

19 The Bread of Life

20 The Light of the World

21 The Door

22 The Good Shepherd

23 The Resurrection and the Life

24 The Way, the Truth and the Life

25 The True Vine

26 Alpha and Omega

27 The Bright and Morning Star

Portrait 19

The Bread of Life

I am the bread of life....

John 6:35

The multitude had witnessed the miracle of the feeding of the five thousand with the loaves and fishes. To escape the press of the crowd, Jesus retired to a mountain and then crossed the lake to the other side. The people followed Him by ship. Their enquiries revealed that they were still looking for His miraculous loaves. However, Jesus pointed to the Giver and said, "I am the bread of life."

In essence, Jesus said that what bread was to the physical life, He was to the soul. How fitting that Jesus was born in Bethlehem which was known as the House of Bread. Bread has been called the staff of life. It is the basic staple for existence. Other foods are expendable, but not bread. Christ is inexpendable to life and sustenance.

Christ discerned that the seeking of the crowd was for the material rather than for the spiritual. He said, "You are not really for me but for the loaves I gave you which you ate and were filled." Do we not find in these words an indictment on contemporary religiosity? Even in what sometimes appears to be our religious duties to Christ we find ulterior motives. Have we not too often observed those who come to church for the bread that perishes? In their coming they are seeking respectability, in their service they are seeking an image of devoutness, in their giving they are seeking personal prestige or trying to compensate for a higher gift required by God. Selfishness can govern even our religious pursuits.

Have we not at times sought the impersonal in religion instead of the personal, the transient instead of the eternal, the shadowy instead of the substantial? Sometimes we try to cultivate the image instead of the reality, forgetting that if we cultivate the reality the image will take care of itself.

The transient pleasures, the phantom charms, the evanescent fame and success are like bubbles. They sparkle, and, like children, we reach out to them only to find that when we grasp them their charm vanishes. The intoxicating cups of the world's pleasures will turn to bitterness. The orgiastic banquets of earthly indulgence will turn to nausea and dissipate life's true values.

Jesus in this chapter was referring to the deepest hunger and thirst of life. There is in man a bias toward his Creator. The psalmist employed a metaphor that would as graphically and as strongly as possible convey this thought when he exclaimed, "As the hart panteth after the water brooks, so panteth my soul after thee, O God. My soul thirsteth for God, for the living God . . ." (Psalms 42:1,2).

On one of those intoxicating Indian Summer days in the Pocono Mountains of Pennsylvania there was suddenly the bounding noise of a deer coming over a knoll and the eerie sound of hunting dogs on the chase. The deer passed close enough so that I could see the desperate look in its eyes, the parched tongue hanging out of the side of its mouth. Down the mountain it ran, outdistancing its pursuers, until it reached the deep ravine and the cold fresh stream cascading over the rocks. How it panted after the water brooks! So in man there is an intense longing, thirsting, hunger for God. There is a thirst that no earthly spring can slake. There is a hunger that no earthly bread can satisfy. Only Christ, who is the Bread of Life, can satisfy the deepest hunger and yearning of the soul.

Bread has to be taken regularly for its nourishing value. Christ, in this discourse, tells His followers that they should eat of this bread. We need to take Christ into our inmost being. We need to assimilate the truths and the reality of His presence into our daily lives. He will sustain us. He will replenish our spent strength and our exhausted store of endurance. He will give vitality and vigor to the spiritual life. There cannot be bread except the grain be bruised, broken, and crushed. Christ sacrificed Himself to become for us the Bread of Life.

O Christ, Thou Bread of Life, satisfy the deepest hungers of my life.

Portrait 20

The Light of the World

I am the light of the world. . . .

John 8:12

What light is to the earth, Jesus is to mankind. Light is indispensable to life. It is a great mystery, yet it is one of man's greatest friends. In many ways physical light is analogous to the One who is the Light of the World.

The world needs light. It cannot exist or survive without it. Darkness and barrenness would prevail without light. Nothing could grow, nothing could live.

The world without Christ is a world of darkness, groping and lost. Without Christ the world is in philosophical darkness. He alone is the fulfillment of the philosopher's quest. Without Christ the world is in sociological darkness. He alone teaches the higher laws of love which contribute to true brotherhood and peace. Without Christ the world is in spiritual darkness. He alone can save man from the deep and dark night of sin.

Light dispels darkness. The darkness cannot remain where there is light. Light makes the darkness flee. Christ, as the Light of the World, dispels the spiritual darkness that would overshadow a life. He lifts us from the shadows. He transfers us from the shady to the sunny side of the street of life. As a sunny day lifts the spirit, so He makes life exhilarating and exuberant by His brightness.

Light is the great revealer. The most beautiful flowers, the most majestic mountains are obscured in inky blackness until they are rescued from the night and bathed in the glorious sunlight. Only then do they thrill us with the wonder of their beauty.

At the Academia in Florence, Italy, we were overwhelmed with the beauty of Michelangelo's great works of sculpture, including his magnificent David. But also of interest were the unfinished statuary which revealed by their chisel marks something of the method of Michelangelo's sculpturing. It recalled to mind his concept that he did not create these works but rather unveiled what was already in the marble, cutting away the superfluities. Thus would he give to the world his Pietà or an angel that he saw in a rough piece of marble. Christ releases from its imprisoned splendor the divine qualities within a life and reveals by His light the otherwise hidden glory and beauty of the divine imprint.

It is so easy to trip up in our spiritual lives. Light guides. In the dark men easily stumble and fall. Light makes possible an intelligent sense of direction and destiny.

Light permeates. It is the fastest thing known to man. It travels at its phantom speed of 186,000 miles a second. It is unhindered by space and time. So Christ transcends the barriers of time and space. He is the Contemporary of every age. He is nearer than our dearest one on earth.

Light is pure. Water may start out as a pure spring but too soon it becomes impure when it comes close to man's habitations. Snow makes contact with earth's impurities when it falls from the sky. The wind and air become contaminated with man's toxic chemicals. But light may shine through the most foul medium and yet come out impeccably pure. So Christ mingled amidst earth's moral pollution and yet remained spotlessly pure. He is the pure Light.

In our meditation on this great title, we must not forget the other side of the coin of this saying. Jesus said, "I am the light of the world." But He also said to His disciples, "Ye are the light of the world" (Matthew 5:14). How do we reconcile these two sayings?

Every student of astronomy knows that there are two orders of luminaries. There is that which is its own source of light. The sun is of this order. Then there is the luminary which has no light of its own. It catches and reflects light from another source. The moon is an example of that kind of luminary. Without the light of the sun it would be a sterile, dark ball in a midnight sky. But catching the radiance of the sun, it becomes a glowing, luminous heavenly body up in our sky. Our light is a borrowed ray from the Sun of Righteousness. How wonderful it is that our dim and dull lives can catch His radiance and reflect it in a darkened world.

Thou source of lustrous lives, help me to catch and reflect Thy radiance and glory.

Portrait 21

The Door

I am the door. . . .

John 10:9

This title refers to the unique custom of the Eastern sheepfold. At night the shepherd would gather the sheep in a stone or other type of natural or improvised enclosure with a narrow opening. Then he himself would lay across that opening and become literally the door of the fold.

A traveler once, when skies were rose and gold
With Syrian sunset, paused beside the fold,
Where an Arabian shepherd housed his flock;
Only a circling wall of rough, gray rock—
No door, no gate, but just an opening wide
Enough for snowy, huddling sheep to come inside.
"So," questioned he, "then no wild beasts you dread?"
"Ah, yes, the wolf is near," the shepherd said.
"But"—strange and sweet the words Divine of yore
Fell on his startled ear: *"I am the door!"*
When skies are sown with stars, and I may trace
The velvet shadows in this narrow space,
I lay me down. No silly sheep may go
Without the fold but I, the shepherd, know.
Nor need my cherished flock, close-sheltered, warm,
Fear ravening wolf, save o'er my prostrate form."
O word of Christ—illumined evermore
For us His timid sheep—"I am the door."

AUTHOR UNKNOWN

Christ is the Door of salvation: "by me if any man enter in, he shall be saved." Many have tried to climb the wall of redemption by vain philosophy, human effort, religious systems—but apart from Christ there is no salvation.

Lew Wallace, author of *Ben Hur,* was challenged by the noted agnostic, Robert G. Ingersoll, to give the world a book that would prove the falsity of Jesus Christ. Wallace spent many years travelling abroad researching ancient manuscripts. But, as he started to write, he realized that all his research had only proved that Jesus Christ was real in history. Then he became more convinced that Christ not only lived but He was divine, resurrected, and was the Saviour of men. At fifty years of age he prayed for the first time and accepted Christ as his Saviour. Then he rewrote his manuscript and gave the world *Ben Hur* to prove that Christ is the Son of God and the Saviour of the world. Christ is the Door of salvation.

Christ is the Door of spiritual freedom. Of the sheep who pass through this door Christ said they "shall go in and out." This suggests activity. There is a coming and going for God. Life has deeper dimensions and broader horizons when we have a Christian perspective. His fold is not a place of confinement. The Christian life is not one of prescription and restriction. It is a life of glorious liberty. The Christian enjoys the abundant life (*see* v.10).

Christ is the Door to a vital and virile life: "he shall find pasture." Life is enriched and enhanced by our communion with Him and our fellowship in the Christian community.

It is implied in this title that Christ is the Door to the fold of God. The true church, or fold, is His mystical body—that company of true followers irrespective of denominational stripe. Through Christ, the Door, we enter and become part of the great flock of God. Christ is the Chief Shepherd and Bishop of our souls.

O Christ the Door, Your titles and my needs fit each other. I thank You for the abundant entrance You have given into the fold of God.

Portrait 22

The Good Shepherd

I am the good shepherd....

John 10:11

In touring the famed St. Calixtus Catacombs in Rome, our attention was captivated by the third-century paintings on the rock walls. They bore a revealing testimony to the life and thought of the early Christian church. We were interested to discover among those rare paintings one of Christ as the Good Shepherd, carrying a sheep over His shoulder. This concept of Christ as the Good Shepherd has perhaps been the most endearing portrait of the Master through the centuries. This picture graces the wall of many Christian homes today. In our transition from rural to urban life, we have not lost the beauty and the meaning of this portrait of our Lord.

What passage of Scripture has been more cherished than the Shepherd Psalm? When I served in a pastoral capacity, it was the one passage I felt I always had to read over the open grave. It was the one that invariably would be shared in the tender and sacred moment by the bedside of the one ready to go to the Father's house. Jesus gave new content and fulfillment to the Shepherd Psalm.

The portrait of the Good Shepherd is delineated in the context of this and other Shepherd passages. The shepherd had an intimate knowledge of his sheep: "He calleth his own sheep by name" (v. 3). "I ... know my sheep, and am known of mine" (v. 14). The shepherd of the Orient had a much more intimate relation with his sheep than the shepherd of the West. In our part of the world sheep are raised mostly for meat. In the East they would be raised for their wool and milk. The shepherd would stay with the sheep sometimes as long as ten years. Thus, the shepherd and sheep would develop a close and tender relationship. The Good Shepherd knows His sheep.

"He goeth before them" (v. 4) portrays the feet of the Good Shepherd. The shepherd did not drive his sheep, he led them. Christ has gone the way before us. He has journeyed through life's thorn-grown wilderness, amidst its deep chasms and plunging precipices. He knows life's dangers and perils. The Good Shepherd leads His sheep "beside the still waters." Otherwise a rushing current might sweep away the flock to destruction, or mask the sound of an approaching enemy. But He does not always lead us in pastures green or by waters still. Sometimes He leads us amid the tempests and storms and down into the deep ravines of life. But there is reassurance and adequacy in the leading and the presence of the Good Shepherd.

"Thy rod and thy staff they comfort me" (Psalms 23:4). These words tell us something about the hands of the shepherd. The rod was a stout piece of wood with which the shepherd fought off the enemies of the sheep. With strength and courage he would beat off the wild beasts or the marauder of the flock. The staff was a long, crooked stick which the shepherd would gently lay on the back of the sheep to keep it from straying and getting lost. There was not only the strength and protection of the shepherd's hands but also their tenderness. "Thou anointest my head with oil" (Psalms 23:5). The strong tender hands of the shepherd would rub oil into the fleece of the sheep. It would be refreshing and soothing. Our Good Shepherd protects us from the deadly enemies of our soul. He refreshes us with the balm of His tender presence.

There is also portrayed the heart of the Good Shepherd. "But when he saw the multitudes, he was moved with compassion on them because they fainted, and were scattered abroad, as sheep having no shepherd" (Matthew 9:36). We are like sheep, often foolish and prone to wander. His was an urgent, active love on our behalf.

In Luke 15:4–6, Jesus likens Himself to the shepherd who had one hundred sheep. Ninety-nine were safe in the fold and one was lost. The shepherd went into the wilderness and sought and found the lost sheep. He brought it back on his shoulders and called his neighbors to celebrate with him, "Rejoice with me; for I have found my sheep which was lost."

The true shepherd would place himself between his flock and the peril. Jesus said, "The Good Shepherd giveth his life for the sheep" (John 10:11). His love for us was so great that He laid down His life to save us.

Our Shepherd will be there beside us when we pass through the "valley of the shadow of death." Then, with the Good Shepherd, we will dwell in our Father's house forevermore.

Good Shepherd, lead me through my life's maze to my Father's house.

Portrait 23

The Resurrection and the Life

I am the resurrection, and the life: he that believeth in me, though he were dead, yet shall he live.

John 11:25

These words were spoken in the midst of a drama of human death and gloom. They were spoken in a situation of heartbreak and agony. This type of agony is well known to the human race, as the tender ties of human affection and association are severed, and there is, in the words of Tennyson, a longing for

> ... the touch of a vanish'd hand,
> And the sound of a voice that is still!

That little home of Bethany that had so often been a retreat and a haven of rest for the Master had now become a morgue of gloom and dismay. Lazarus had died. There was the deep grief of the sisters and friends, and the plaintive wailing of the mourners.

In this darkest of settings Jesus gives us one of His most radiant titles. Many consider this the climax of His "I Am" statements. It is a supreme and superlative expression of His authority over life and death.

At least four times while on earth Jesus demonstrated His authority over death. First, there was Jairus's daughter, the maid or young child that had been snatched by the grim reaper at so tender an age (Matthew 9:23–26). Then there was the only son of the widow of Nain that was being carried out on the bier. Jesus in His compassion spoke those precious words of life, "Young man, I say unto thee, Arise" (Luke 7:12–16). Then there were the dramatic words of our text spoken to the one who had been dead four days and would by then stink with the fetid smell of human death. In one of the most climactic moments of Bible narrative, Jesus calls, "Lazarus, come forth" (John 11:43) and the dead man comes forth from the tomb still bound in his grave clothes. Finally there was His own mighty Resurrection which gave ultimate confirmation and authority to His majestic words, "I am the resurrection and the life" (John 11:25).

There was the day when Jesus was in the tomb. Hearts were heavy. The crestfallen disciples on the Emmaus road represented the dismay of all followers at what seemed to be the defeat of Christ and the coming to naught of all His wonderful claims. Death had claimed Him as a victim and snuffed out the hope that had sprung from His radiant promises.

In the history of man, there was another momentous day that seemed ominous with defeat. When the decisive battle of Waterloo was fought, the people of London anxiously awaited news of the outcome of battle. In those days messages were sent by means of semaphore signals. From the top of Winchester Cathedral the people saw and read the message, "Wellington defeated" and then a blanket of fog veiled the signalers. The people of London were in deep despair at the thought of their great general being defeated. All seemed lost. But later that day the fog lifted and again the message was being signaled. Again they read, "Wellington defeated"—but this time there was more to the message until they read, "Wellington defeated the enemy." Gloom changed to glory, despair to delight, tragedy had become triumph. So, too, when the fog had lifted following Calvary, the glorious message passed like wildfire, "He is risen!" and defeat was changed into victory. Christ became the great victor over death instead of its victim. Christ the Mighty Conqueror came and cut the Gordian knot of death by the decisive thrust of His Resurrection.

Jesus destroyed the last enemy of death. He took the sting out of it. The little girl whose path from school led through a graveyard was asked if she were afraid and replied, "Oh, no, I just cross it to reach home." That is parabolic of what Jesus had done for us in regard to His conquest over death.

But there are two sides of the coin of this text. Christ is not only the Resurrection of death but He is also the Life for us here. Christ is our source of true life here as well as hereafter. He rescues life from becoming inane. He redeems it from being merely existence. The Life He gives has to be spelled with a capital *L*. He gives qualitative dimension to life, making it supremely significant and purposeful.

Thou who art the Resurrection and the Life, keep me ever under the spell of immortality.

Portrait 24

The Way, the Truth, and the Life

Jesus saith unto him, I am the way, the truth, and the life.
John 14:6

The setting of our text is the Upper Room, and this fourteenth chapter of John is part of our Lord's farewell discourse to His disciples. He has just said some astonishing things. He has spoken of His Father's house and mansions and going away where the disciples would not be able to follow. These mystical statements are too much for Thomas with his practical bent of mind. As one of our Lord's ardent followers he asks, "How can we know the way?" This question comes echoing down the centuries. More than ever, man today is lost in the labyrinthine maze of life and is crying out, "How can we know the way?"

There are so many ways that beckon and so many voices that clamor for our attention and allegiance. Hinduism calls to the people of India, Shintoism to the people of Japan, Zoroastrianism to the people of Persia, Confucianism and Taoism to the people of China, Islam to the people of the Moslem countries. Communism with its dialectic materialism says Marxism and its godless, classless society is the way. To many, science seems a panacea for the world's ills. In a world of sharply conflicting ideologies, how can we know the way?

Most of us who drive have had the experience of looking for some location. We have stopped to ask a person for directions. His complicated instructions have sometimes overtaxed our memory as well as our imagination. But there have been times when we have asked and a person has said, "Follow me. I am going that way and I will take you there." What a difference when we have had someone who has known the way and has guided us there. The Psalmist said, "Thou wilt show me the path of life" (Psalms 16:11). Jesus does not hand us an impossible creed as the road map for life, but rather He says, "I am the way." He becomes our guide.

Christ did not say He is a way among many other ways. He said, "I am THE way." He is the only way. All other roads are dead ends.

In our text Christ also declares, "I am . . . the truth." Pilate's question, "What is truth?" seems more pertinent in our day than ever. We are so often confronted with diametrically opposed philosophies and claims. What sage or Solomon of today can discern "what is truth?"

In His response to our search for truth, Christ does not give us a precept but a Person; not a what, but a who; not a code or a creed, but His own character. Christ Himself was the standard that would determine truth. He was the embodiment of truth. He was Truth Incarnate.

Truth validates Christ and Christ validates truth. Not one single fact has ever been discovered which invalidates one word of Christ or one aspect of our faith in Him. The true discoveries of science have corroborated Christ. We have discovered that His laws are written not only in the texts of Scripture but into the very texture of life and in the reality of things.

Jesus reveals to us the truth about God, ourselves, and our world. When He was born, wise men came from the East to worship Him. Wise men still come to the One who is Wisdom Incarnate to learn the truth about the meaning and mystery of life. Christ is the *summum bonum* of the philosopher's quest. He is the truth that satisfies the deep yearnings of the intellect.

The final title of this superb trilogy is, "I am the life." Christ is the source of all life. The life in our cosmos is derived from the provision and providence of Christ and the Father. From Him we also receive our spiritual life. Our soul and spirit are energized by Him to live, grow, and go on to life eternal.

> O Christ the Way, lead me, for without Thee there is no going; O Christ the Truth, illumine me, for without Thee there is no knowing; O Christ the Life, live in and through me, for without Thee there is no growing.

Portrait 25

The True Vine

I am the true vine....

John 15:1

It is possible that this allegory was suggested by the sight of vineyards on the way from the Upper Room to the Garden of Gethsemane. Vineyards were common in that part of the world. Five of Christ's parables refer to them. The vine appeared on Jewish coinage, was often carved on the door of a synagogue and according to Josephus was the symbol carved upon the great door of the Temple. The vine was interwoven in the life and thought of His hearers.

There is a twofold concept in this parable. Christ is the Vine. We are the branches. It indicates the most intimate and vital union. The branch draws its very life from the vine. It is intertwined with it and partakes its very nature from the vine. The soul is ingrafted into Christ. The Christian confidently sings, "My soul is now united to Christ the Living Vine."

In His high priestly prayer our Lord prayed, "That they all may be one; as thou, Father, art in me, and I in thee, that they also may be one in us" (John 17:21). Is not this spiritual union with Christ one of the wonders of the Christian life? It was the magnificent obsession of Paul. This myriad-minded professor of the Christian faith no less than 164 times in his thirteen epistles uses the phrase or its equivalent, "In Christ."

There takes place a union of wills. There is a fusion of our will with God's will. The conflict of life is basically a conflict of wills—man's will in conflict with God's will. Victory comes when man's will is surrendered to God.

There is also a union of purpose. When united to Christ we are no longer divided personalities suffering the dichotomy of the carnal and the spiritual natures. We live to fulfill His holy purpose for our life.

This union is conditional. Christ said, "If ye abide in me" (John 15:7). There are many things that would interpose themselves between the vine and the branches. There are forces that would break the union and rob the branch of its life-giving power from the Vine. The writer of the Song of Solomon enjoined, "Take us the foxes, the little foxes, that spoil the vines: for our vines have tender grapes" (2:15). Often the little things spoil the luster and richness of life. The little foxes of uncontrolled temper, undisciplined desires, debilitating lethargy, careless talk, often spoil the vineyard of our lives. For indeed the grapes of life are tender and are easily spoiled.

Union with Christ the Vine also involves a purging. "He purgeth it" (John 15:2), says Christ of the fruitful branch. The Greek verb *kathairo* denotes the basic idea of purity. To abide in Christ involves a purifying of heart and life. We must be weaned from all lesser loves, cleansed from selfishness, and sanctified by His Spirit. Too many Christians seem content with spiritual mediocrity. The vine was more extensively pruned than any other tree, often to the very stump. But the more the dead branches were cut off and the greater the pruning or purging, the more vigorous and fruitful the growth. When life is purged of dead things then it will manifest its most virile life in Christ.

The union of the branch with the vine was also productive of fruit.

The products of the vine from the Jerusalem area were prized throughout the world for their rich taste and quality. There is a spiritual fecundity and fertility that results from union with Christ. A mature tree is a fruit-bearing tree. There is the fruit of the Spirit which is the fruit of Christlike character (*see* Galatians 5:22,23). There is also the fruit of service.

Christ, the True Vine, I would be united to You as the branch is to the vine. Purge my spirit of all dead things and make me fruitful for You.

Portrait 26

Alpha and Omega

I am Alpha and Omega. the beginning and the end, the first and the last.

Revelation 22:13

Here in the closing chapter of the Bible we have, first of all, a portrait of the divinity of Jesus Christ. He here assumes a title which God used in reference to Himself in Revelation 1:8; 21:6.

Furthermore, it reveals the transcendental superiority of Jesus Christ over time. "I am Alpha and Omega." Those two words are the first and last letters of the Greek alphabet. Their significance is explicit in the amplification Jesus Himself gives in this verse: "the beginning and the end, the first and the last."

He is *Alpha,* the Beginning, the First. What a staggering claim! First—before the empires of Egypt, Babylon, Greece, Rome. First—before the eons of time spoken of by geologists. First—before the solar system, the Milky Way, the Pleiades.

We live under the tyranny of time. Jesus is the Master of time. He had no beginning and will have no end. Our seemingly long history on earth represents only an episode in eternity. "For a thousand years in thy sight are but as yesterday when it is past, and as a watch in the night" (Psalms 90:4).

He is *Omega,* the End, the Last. What a blessed assurance. He is not dead. He has not retired from the world. He will be the conclusion. Although Dante's great work was filled with eschatological tragedy, he entitled it, *The Divine Comedy,* because of his belief that in the end God would give happiness to His people. Because Jesus Christ is the End as well as the Beginning, *Omega* as well as *Alpha,* eternal felicity will be the conclusion for His people.

Eternal Christ, be the *Alpha* and *Omega* in my life. Be in all my beginnings, and in my ending.

Portrait 27

The Bright and Morning Star

I am . . . the bright and morning star.

Revelation 22:16

Immanuel Kant wrote: "Two things fill the mind with ever new and increasing wonder and awe—the starry heavens above me and the moral law within me." My favorite sight in nature is the spectacle of a star-bejeweled sky on a dark night. It is a sublime sight and fills the soul with reverence to contemplate not only the beauty of the stars but their fathomless distance and their titanic size. If the stars could be seen only once in every hundred years, it would be the greatest celebration of the century. Every person would stay up all night to drink in the beauty of the sight.

Working with youth, it has been my opportunity on a number of occasions to introduce a boy to the beauty of the stars. It was always a precious moment of discovery and awe such as, "I never knew there were so many stars." In our highly urbanized life, very few people ever really see the stars. But every person of Christ's day immediately had a picture in mind when Christ said, "I am the bright and morning star." The stars figured prominently in the life of the Eastern traveler.

The morning star heralds the dawn of a new day. Christ ushered in a new age. His coming split time in two. His life gave promise of a new and bright future. He came to irradiate this present life. He would also have us look over the horizon of eternity where our chapter tells us, "And there shall be no night there; and they need no candle, neither light of the sun; for the Lord God giveth them light: and they shall reign for ever and ever" (Revelation 22:5).

On several fishing trips up in the north woods of Canada, we drove through the night. It was always interesting to see the gradual approach of dawn in the sky in that area where no electric lights or buildings obscured the view of the stars. The stars of the sky would gradually give way to the light until finally there was only one star shining. All others had faded from view except for the morning star which still shone brightly.

Christ, as the Bright and Morning Star, shines brightly when all other stars of our life fade away. Those things which now shine so brightly on the horizon of our life will someday fade and vanish away. The stars of prestige, position, possessions, and persons dear to us will one by one grow dim and fade away. But after everything else has vanished, Christ will still shine brightly. He will shine on in the darkest night and will radiantly beam over the horizon of life when the dawn breaks and the shadows flee away.

As the morning star is the brightest star in the sky, so is Christ the most radiant light ever to shine in our world. All other luminaries pale into insignificance compared to the brilliance of His life. He is the Peerless One of all history.

For many centuries, man charted his journeys by the stars. Sailors navigated the seas with their eyes on the stars. The stars were the road maps, the directional signs for their times. They would make their way over the tractless wilderness by the guidance they found in the stars.

An artist once drew a picture of a lone man rowing his little boat on a dark night. The wind is fierce; the waves crest and rage around his frail bark. But there is one star that shines through the dark and angry sky above. Upon that star the voyager fixes his eye and keeps rowing on through the storm. Beneath the picture are the words, "If I lose that I'm lost." From Christ alone can we take bearings for our journey on the sea of life. Our boat is small and the sea is so wide. But the compass needle of life will cease its oscillations when its directional point is turned toward the One who is the Bright and Morning Star. Like a mariner, we may reckon all our decisions and directions from that Star.

O radiant Christ, guide my life over the tractless pilgrimage it must make.

IV
The Ministry

Names and Titles Associated With the Life and Ministry of Jesus Christ

- 28 Nazarene
- 29 Son of Man
- 30 Prophet
- 31 Carpenter

- 32 Word
- 33 Lamb of God
- 34 Christ
- 35 Saviour
- 36 God
- 37 Our Passover
- 38 Rock
- 39 The Last Adam
- 40 Chief Corner Stone

- 41 The Head of the Church
- 42 Lord
- 43 Image of the Invisible God
- 44 Firstborn of Every Creature
- 45 Mediator
- 46 The King of Kings
- 47 Heir of All Things
- 48 Apostle of Our Profession
- 49 The Pioneer of Our Faith
- 50 High Priest
- 51 Advocate
- 52 Lion of the Tribe of Judah

Portrait 28

Nazarene

And he came and dwelt in a city called Nazareth: that it might be fulfilled which was spoken by the prophets, He shall be called a Nazarene.

Matthew 2:23

This title of Christ is derived from the small village where He lived during those silent years. The village of Nazareth was quite insignificant. It is not mentioned with other cities in the ancient records of writers. We recall Nathanael's reply of incredulity when Philip told him that the Messiah had come from Nazareth, "Can there any good thing come out of Nazareth?" (John 1:46). Thus was Nazareth thought of and spoken of with contempt. That is, until Jesus changed all that.

In this somewhat obscure village, Jesus grew up. There were brothers and sisters in the home. Jesus played the older brother's part. James and Joses and Juda and Simon would often be helped by their older brother Jesus. It was He who would shepherd them or their sisters through the busy streets and keep them from the danger of the racing chariots. Often He would run errands for His mother. There was water to be brought from the well or a fire to bank on a chilly night. Then there was that desolate day when He, as the older brother, put His strong arms around His mother Mary. Joseph the good father of that family was laid to rest. As the older brother, He stepped into the work of the carpenter's shop and supported the family by the trade He had learned at His father's side.

Christ as the Nazarene lived in a humble home, did the manual work of a carpenter, and mingled in the busy mart and everyday life of the people. There are many to whom this warm portrait of the Master gives comfort and reassurance.

Important caravan routes came through the vicinity of Nazareth. The village residents would witness the throngs of pilgrims on the road from Jerusalem, the wealthy merchants coming up from Egypt, the caravans of the Midianites with their interesting wares. These travelers would echo the news of the world. Thus, as Christ grew, He would be exposed and sensitized to the busy commerce of life. Although Nazareth was not a notable town it was strategically placed amidst the traffic of life in that day. A boy growing up there could see and hear and sense the pulse of the Eastern world.

Nazareth was just a hamlet, obscure and insignificant until Jesus came and made His home there. His presence has a transforming influence on all that comes in close contact with Him. So, too, if we will invite Him to come and make His abode in our life, He will transform its insignificance to eternal meaning and purpose. The devotional words of Stanley Ditmer's song, "The Nazarene," beautifully describe this truth:

> I never knew how poor was my condition,
> For I was blind, and all my need unseen;
> Until one day in my unworthy station,
> I chanced to meet the lowly Nazarene.
>
> It was His life that purchased my salvation;
> It was His grace that set my spirit free.
> It is His Blood that seals my consecration;
> It is His love that intercedes for me.

O Christ, who experienced the common things of humanity, take the drab and broken threads of my everyday life and with

the skill of Your hands weave them into a tapestry of beauty for eternity.

Portrait 29

Son of Man

Even as the Son of man came not to be ministered unto, but to minister, and to give his life a ransom for many.

Matthew 20:28

Jesus used this title of Himself about eighty times in the Gospels. One other time it is used in the Gospels and it is also found in Acts 7:56. Thus, it is the title Jesus selected for Himself. It seems to have its origin in the messianic passage of Daniel 7:13,14:

> I saw in the night visions, and, behold, one like the Son of man came with the clouds of heaven, and came to the Ancient of days, and they brought him near before him.
> And there was given him dominion, and glory, and a kingdom, that all people, nations, and languages should serve him: his dominion is an everlasting dominion, which shall not pass away, and his kingdom that which shall not be destroyed.

This title speaks of the humanity of Jesus Christ. He was God who became man. He was God clothed in the garb of humanity. What unfathomable love! What condescension! That God should take upon Himself the frailty and the limitation of man. The One who had spoken oceans into existence became a man and asked an outcast for a drink. The Infinite became Intimate.

At the Pitti Art Gallery in Florence, Italy, a guide was comparing portrait paintings of the Renaissance. Pointing to one that was unobscured by extraneous detail, she said, "Now this portrait looks as though you can converse with Him." When leaving Florence, a woman on the train remarked to us, "Christ and the apostles seem so much more real since I've seen these pictures." This portrait of Christ as the Son of man makes Him real to our understanding. He steps out of the pages of the New Testament as One who entered into the common lot of our humanity. We see Him weary, hungry, thirsting, laughing, conversing, weeping, suffering, dying.

This title is associated not only with the humanity of Jesus Christ but with His divinity as well. We cannot neatly compartmentalize His humanity. He was a mysterious and majestic composite of man and God. This title is linked with some of the sublime declarations of Christ. Among them:

> When the Son of man shall come in his glory, and all the holy angels with him, then shall he sit upon the throne of his glory. And before him shall be gathered all nations; and he shall separate them one from another . . . (Matthew 25:31,32).
> Hereafter you will see the Son of man seated at the right hand of power, and coming in the clouds of heaven (Matthew 26:64; Mark 14:62; *see* Luke 22:69).

Our text at the beginning reminds us of Christ's mission as the Son of man. It was a role assumed to serve (to minister), to suffer (give His life), and to save (ransom for many).

Christ of the human road, walk with me and help me in my humanity to ever be linked with Your divinity.

Portrait 30

Prophet

"And the multitude said, This is Jesus the prophet of Nazareth of Galilee."

Matthew 21:11

To the devout believer of biblical days, prophets were of the highest rank and order among men. When awed by His miracles or witnessing a demonstration of His deep wisdom or great power, people often acclaimed Him a prophet. It was the highest compliment that would be given to a man.

A prophet was specially chosen and anointed by God. God vouchsafed His message to man through the prophets. The prophet was God's mouthpiece. He had two primary functions: He foretold the future and He forthtold God's message to man. Each prophet of the Old Testament gave some new insight concerning God. Isaiah's sublime passages reveal God's holiness and give incomparable predictions of the coming Messiah; Jeremiah reveals the significance of personal religion; through Hosea God bares His heart of forgiveness for the backslider; Amos thundered God's declarations for the application of religion to the ills of society, to mention but a few.

Jesus supremely fulfilled the office of a prophet. His teachings and revealings were the culmination and the grand denouement of prophetical utterance. But Jesus was more than a prophet. He was the fulfillment of the prophecies that had gone before. Other prophets had been called and commissioned to prepare the way for Him. He was the Sun of Righteousness toward which all their flickering torches pointed. Viewing Christ as a prophet was a window to His greatness through which we could gain a greater and grander view of His supernal qualities.

My reading experience was once greatly enriched by a biography of Tennyson with the noteworthy title: *The Preeminent Victorian.* Other than Queen Victoria herself, no one else could be given that title. His life spanned almost all the Victorian Age. As Poet Laureate, he was the voice of that era. But there is a restrictive characteristic to that title. Tennyson belonged to his age. Christ belongs to the ages. Tennyson was considered preeminent for that period. Christ is the Preeminent One for all ages and eras. Compared to His brightness and glory all other prophets were as a flashing meteorite which appears briefly on the horizon and quickly burns itself out. He transcends the prophets and fulfills their God-given oracles.

Thou preeminent Christ, rule and reign over all else in my heart and life.

Portrait 31

Carpenter

Is not this the carpenter. . . ?

Mark 6:3

The word for carpenter is the word *tekton* which meant an artisan, a craftsman, one who was a builder.

The Scriptures reveal Christ as a Carpenter of the universe: "All things were made by him; and without him was not any thing made that was made" (John 1:3). The hands that held the hammer and worked the saw here on earth were hands that carpentered the fathomless galaxies and the infinite depths of creation. Those hands that shaved and smoothed the wood at the carpenter's bench in Nazareth also created the stars and the planets with their perfect design and precision.

The Cosmic Carpenter by the miracle of the Incarnation became the Carpenter of Nazareth. The question of our text asked by the disaffected Nazarenes on that Sabbath day is the only window in the Scriptures through which we may look upon the years of His young manhood. These few words speak volumes to us about the silent years. This portrait of our Lord as a carpenter suggests many things that would characterize His daily round of toil.

The absence of Joseph from the later Gospel narratives seems to suggest that the wise and humble father of that family had been laid to rest, and Jesus, as the elder brother, took over the support of the family by the trade He had mastered in His father's shop. Then finally, when the other brothers and sisters were old enough, He made His last yoke. After shaking the wood shavings from His tunic for the last time, He went out to build the eternal Kingdom of God in the hearts of men.

This portrait of Christ as a Carpenter identifies Him with mankind. How reassuring it is to know that He who now holds a scepter in His hand once held a hammer and a saw. It is a vivid portrait of the manhood of Jesus Christ. Often His hands would be bruised and torn by the grain. As He worked day after day, making the wood obedient to His skill, His hands became as strong as a vise. They became roughened and callused, the kind of hands strong fishermen would look at and know that they could follow Him with confidence and respect. He knew the meaning of toil. He understands our burdens, our weariness, our tasks.

As the Carpenter, Christ forever sanctified human toil. No man is an island. We are all members of the corporate society. As we derive many benefits so must we be contributive to the community. There is a self-fulfillment in doing a job that contributes to the ongoing of community life. No such task should be considered menial. It was given dignity by the One who worked amid the wood shavings at the carpenter's bench for the greater part of His life. His labor enabled the oxen to plow without being chafed by their yokes, children to take delight in the hand-carved toys, families to live in the comfort of a home built by the Carpenter.

Today, the Carpenter of Nazareth who once smoothed yokes in His skillful hands, would take a life that is yielded to Him and fashion it into a beautiful and useful instrument of God's eternal Kingdom.

Thou Carpenter of Nazareth, take my life and smooth the coarseness of its grain, work out the flaws and imperfections, make me a worthwhile and useful instrument for the Kingdom.

Portrait 32

Word

In the beginning was the Word, and the Word was with God, and the Word was God.

John 1:1

. . . His name is called The Word of God.

Revelation 19:13

History has proven that the pen is often more powerful than the sword. Words have swayed empires, preserved the freedom of embattled peoples, drastically altered the course of history. Words are also an index to the person who utters them. They reveal how vivid is the person's encounter with life, how vibrant is the personality behind them.

The Greeks had three words for *word*. One meant the sound of a voice, another was a sound revealing a mental state, and the third is the one of our text. It is one of the great words of the Greek New Testament—*logos*. *Logos* combines the thought of expression and wisdom. It means a word which embodies a concept or idea. This rich word is not easily translatable into English. Thus Moffatt leaves it untranslated and renders our text:

The Logos existed in the very beginning,
the Logos was with God,
the Logos was divine.

As the Word, Christ was God become *vocal*. "God, who . . . spake in time past unto the fathers by the prophets, Hath in these last days spoken unto us by his Son" (Hebrew 1:1,2). Gone were the days when men would determine God's will by the quaint method of the Urim and Thummin. No longer would human prophets give a gradual unfolding of the divine message. God would speak His great and glorious message through His Son. Christ became the ultimate medium of communication from God to man. Through Christ, God spoke to man in a new and living language—the language of life in Christ.

Our text in Revelation speaks of the Word as having His robe dipped in blood. We are reminded that He spoke God's message most eloquently in His sacrifice and death. The cross was the bulletin board on which God proclaimed to the world His amnesty for rebellious sinners.

As the Word, Christ was God become *visible*. A word reveals. It is the revelation of the thought or concept in the mind of another. Although centuries separate us from Milton and Tennyson and Shakespeare, their words reveal their thoughts and their philosophies. As the Word of God, Christ portrays the mind and heart of God. He unveils the mysterious, mighty, magnificent, and majestic God. He makes the transcendent God of the universe immanent upon earth to man.

In Rome there is the elegant fresco known as the *Aurora* by Guido. It covers a lofty ceiling. As one attempts to observe it from below, the neck becomes stiff, the head dizzy, and the figures indistinct. But the owner of the palace has placed a large mirror near the floor. Thus the tourist may now sit before the mirror and, looking into it, enjoy the fresco that is above. So Christ mirrors for us the otherwise inaccessible and invisible Cosmic Presence above us. He reveals and discloses God to man.

In the breathtaking prologue to his Gospel, John declares five stupendous truths about the Word: (1) His eternity—"In the beginning"; (2) His fellowship in the Godhead—"with God"; (3) His deity—"was God"; (4) His work in creation—"All things were made by him"; (5) His marvelous Incarnation—"was made flesh."

A few years before the death of Christ, Philo, an Alexandrian Jew, fused the Greek and Jewish thought on this word *logos* and wrote extensively on it, clothing it with a metaphysical conception. Thus, this word came to have more extensive and significant currency, communicating effectively to both Jewish and Greek thought. But Christ was bigger even than this great word and filled it with new meaning.

> Who dies with Thee, O Word divine,
> Shall rise and live again.
> ALBERT ORSBORN

Thou Living Word, Revealer of God and Communicator of man, help me to know the Eternal Presence as a living and bright reality.

Portrait 33

Lamb of God

Behold the Lamb of God which taketh away the sin of the world.
John 1:29

The portrait that John gives to us of Christ as the Lamb of God has its roots in the sacrificial system of the Jews. There were four kinds of sacrifices they offered to God: (1) libations or drink-offerings, (2) savor or incense-offerings, (3) vegetable or meal-offerings, and (4) animal-offerings. They are broadly classified as bloodless and bloody sacrifices. The animal sacrifices were distinguished as burnt-offering, sin-offering, peace-offering, and guilt-offering. Thus it was that upon the altar of the Temple there was always ascending the smoke from a carefully selected lamb or other innocent victim. Man realized that his guilt required expiation by blood. This was dramatically underscored in the unacceptable offering by Cain in contrast to the blood offering of Abel.

When Adam and Eve sinned we read that God Himself clothed them with the skins of animals (*see* Genesis 3:21). To do this it was necessary that some animal, perhaps a lamb, had to shed its blood to cover their shame. God declared in the Levitical Code that ". . . it is the blood that maketh an atonement for the soul" (Leviticus 17:11). So this scarlet thread is woven throughout the Old Testament until it takes us to Calvary's altar where we see the perfect Lamb of God sacrificed for the sins of the world. Never again would it be necessary for a lamb to be slain for the sins of man.

Not all the animals slain on Jewish altars would bring peace to the guilty conscience or wash away man's stain of sin. But Christ as the Heavenly Lamb, of noble sacrifice and divine blood, cleanses the sinner and makes him whole.

The Prince of the Prophets in the Old Testament graphically described the Lamb of God:

> He was oppressed, and he was afflicted,
> Yet he opened not his mouth:
> He is brought as a lamb to the slaughter,
> And as a sheep before her shearers is dumb,
> So he openeth not his mouth.
> Isaiah 53:7

In the New Testament, Peter reminds us that we were not redeemed with corruptible things but rather ". . . with the precious blood of Christ, as of a lamb without blemish and without spot" (1 Peter 1:19).

From Adam all mankind has the heirloom of original sin. For this universal problem the sacrifice of Christ is the universal remedy.

But someone asks, "How can the sacrifice of one avail for all?" The answer is in the worth of the One who made the sacrifice. When Christ sacrificed Himself as the Lamb of God, it was not an ordinary man that died. It was God Himself. Thus His sacrifice has infinite merit.

In the last book of the Bible, Christ is portrayed as the Lamb no less than twenty-nine times by John the Seer. But it is not the familiar figure found in the fourth Gospel. In fact, a different word is used for *lamb* and Christ is portrayed as the exalted Lamb of God at the celestial throne that has accomplished the redemption of God's people. May we one day gather with that innumerable host around the throne of God and raise our voice in the great doxology to the Lamb of God: "Worthy is the Lamb that was slain to receive power, and riches, and wisdom, and strength, and honour, and glory, and blessing" (Revelation 5:12).

Dear Lamb of God, I thank You for Your great sacrifice that avails for my guilt and sin.

Portrait 34

Christ

... We have found the Messias, which is, being interpreted, the Christ.

John 1:41

In our listing of titles in the Old Testament we included the *Messiah*. *Christ* is the Greek equivalent of the Hebrew *Messiah*. It means the *Anointed One*. Our chapter on the Old Testament title related to it in prophecy whereas our title in the New Testament relates to it in fulfillment.

This title was especially associated with prophecy. Throughout the Old Testament there were many prophetical utterances concerning the Messiah or God's Anointed One who should come. He is the Seed of the Woman in Genesis, the Star and Sceptre in Numbers, the Redeemer in Job, the Rose of Sharon in the Song of Solomon, the Servant of God in Isaiah, the Lord of Righteousness in Jeremiah, the Messiah in Daniel, the Desire of All Nations in Haggai, the King in Zechariah and the Messenger of the Covenant in Malachi.

Not only was the Messiah prophesied to come, but there were particularized many aspects about His coming. The city where He would be born, the heralding work of John the Baptist, His sojourn in Egypt, His type of ministry, His betrayal, death, and Resurrection were all graphically foretold in many minute details that only Christ could fulfill.

The story is told of Penelope, being annoyed by suitors after Ulysses had been gone ten years. Thinking him to be dead she at last promised to marry the one who should shoot an arrow through twelve rings with the bow Ulysses had used. In the meantime, Ulysses arrived disguised as a beggar and came to the place of trial. One by one the suitors stepped forth but found they were unable to bend the bow. Then spoke Ulysses, "Beggar as I am, I was once a soldier and there is still some strength in these old limbs of mine, let me try." The suitors jeered him, but Penelope consented for him to try. With ease he bent the bow, adjusted the cord to its notch and sped the arrow unerring through the rings. It was Ulysses! Penelope threw herself into his arms.

It was not enough for Christ to claim to be the Messiah. There were many claimants to the Messiahship. But He proved by His credentials in fulfilling the divine prophecies that He was indeed the Messiah. He is irrefutably the unerring fulfillment of the messianic prophecies. Not one of them fail to fit His life and ministry. Every Old Testament reference to the Messiah validates Christ's breathtaking claim, "I am He" (*see* John 4:26).

The Messiah was the One greatly longed for among the Jews. At about the time Jesus was born, there was especially an air of expectancy because of the time foretold by the prophets that the Messiah would come. Thus the statement of the Samaritan woman, "I know that Messias cometh, which is called Christ" (v. 25). Thus the elated announcement by Andrew to his brother Peter, "We have found the Messias" (John 1:41). The Sanhedrin demanded of Him, "Art thou the Christ?" (Luke 22:67).

The story is told of a woman who lived alone in the hills of the South and had all along her living-room walls pictures of Robert E. Lee. One night in a snowstorm two men came and stopped at her house for temporary shelter. Upon leaving, one of the men, very distinguished in appearance, gave her a little gift. The woman asked the other man the name of her distinguished and kind guest. He replied, "That, ma'm, is General Robert E. Lee." Although she had his pictures she did not recognize him when he came.

The Messiah was portrayed in the Old Testament and the prophecies were known to every devout Jew. Yet most did not recognize and accept Him as the Messiah when He came. Their concept was too selfish, materialistic, and nationalistic instead of spiritual.

O Christ, fulfull Thy gracious and great purposes in my life.

Portrait 35

Saviour

> *. . . this is indeed the Christ, the Saviour of the world."*
> John 4:42

This title was not a new word to the ancient world. Egyptian kings were called Saviours. Some of the Roman emperors were designated by this title. But Jesus took this title and gave it new and external meaning.

In the New Testament this title is found most in 2 Peter where it is used of Christ five times. Peter knew Christ well as Saviour. There was that time when recklessly he started to walk out on the waves of the sea and, when suddenly his faith and then his foothold failed, he desperately cried out to Christ to save him. But there were other tempests from which Peter was rescued by Christ. There were the tempests within, when he was prone to base denial and faithlessness, and Christ saved him from disaster. Peter's steps seemed especially to be dogged by Satan who as a roaring lion sought to devour him, but his Master saved him. This became one of Peter's favorite titles for his Lord who had rescued him from so much.

When Lincoln's body was brought back by train to Springfield, Illinois, a former slave held her little child up to see the flag-draped casket containing the great emancipator's body. She said to her child: "Take a long look, honey. That's the man who died to set us free." The title *Saviour* speaks of Christ's great sacrifice to save us from sin —its guilt, power, condemnation, eternal death.

At the Berlin World Congress on Evangelism in 1966, delegates were deeply moved by the testimony of Kimo. Kimo was one of the Auca killers of missionaries eleven years before in the jungle of interior Ecuador. When asked in an interview: "What has Jesus done to change your life?" he answered: "I don't live the same way I did before. I don't live sinning now. Now I live speaking to God." Thus world leaders on evangelism witnessed a classic example of Christ's mighty salvation in the twentieth century.

There was once a gravestone which read, "Sacred to the memory of Methuselah Coney, who died aged six months." A name with a great meaning but unfortunately not fulfilled in the life of Methuselah Coney. There was no correspondence between the infant and the connotation of his name. Others in history had been called Saviour, but Christ alone was able to measure up to the full meaning of this title.

>   I know a soul that is steeped in sin,
>   That no man's art can cure;
>   But I know a Name, a Name, a Name,
>   That can make that soul all pure.
>
>   I know a life that is lost to God,
>   Bound down by things of earth;
>   But I know a Name, a Name, a Name,
>   That can bring that soul new birth.
>
>   I know of lands that are sunk in shame,
>   Of hearts that faint and tire;

> But I know a Name, a Name, a Name,
> That will set those lands on fire.
> AUTHOR UNKNOWN

Dear Saviour, in Thee I would be born twice so that I will die but once, rather than to be born but once and die twice.

Portrait 36

God

And Thomas answered and said unto him, My Lord and my God.
John 20:28

In his devotional classic, Isaac Watts leads us to exclaim in sacred song:

> Amazing love! How can it be
> That Thou, my God, shouldst die for me?

The divinity of Jesus Christ is the cornerstone of Christian theology. This belief is attested by Scripture.

In Philippians 2:6, Paul writes of Christ: "Who, being in the form of God." The word for *form* in the original Greek text is *morphe*. It was a Greek philosophical term meaning more than shape. It permanently identifies Christ with the nature and character of God. The word denotes that the essential nature of divinity comes from within and is permanently a part of Him.

In contrast, Paul states in Philippians 2:8 that Christ was "found in fashion as a man." The Greek word for *fashion* is *schema* and denotes that which is assumed from the outside and does not come from within the essential nature. Our Lord's divinity came from His inmost and essential nature, whereas His manhood was assumed from the outside.

John, who had the most intimate contact with Christ, declares that in Christ the "Word was God" (John 1:1). Thomas who was a Palestinian with a practical bent of mind, upon seeing the risen Christ testified, "My Lord and my God." Paul makes a superlative statement in Colossians 2:9, "For in him dwelleth all the fulness of the Godhead bodily." In his epistle to Titus, Paul writes: "Looking for that blessed hope, and the glorious appearing of the great God and our Saviour Jesus Christ" (2:13).

History also attests to the divinity of Jesus Christ. Emerson said that the name of Christ is not written but plowed into history. Jesus lived and preached in a state about the size of New Hampshire. The crowds who heard Him were much smaller than those who attend a political convention today. But history could not obscure Him. Palestine could not confine Him even though He was put to death as a criminal upon a cross.

One of our most moving experiences was our visit to the Coliseum in Rome. We went there several evenings late at night and just mused in that place of sacred history. We tried to envision the scene of the ferocious beasts mauling the Christians amidst the derision of the bloodthirsty crowd. We noted that in that very place is erected a cross that enshrines and endears the memory of those who were martyrs for their faith. The Coliseum today and what it represents is but a shadow of what once it was. But on the dust of Rome's fallen glory and upon the ashes of her vanished splendor, Christ has built His imperishable church. He towers over the wrecks of time and transcends all eras and splendors of history.

The divinity of Jesus Christ is further corroborated by personal experience. A man newly converted was chided at work: "Now don't tell me you believe that story about Jesus turning water into wine?" The man replied, "I don't know about that, but I can tell you that in from this tenement of clay lest its fermentative process corrupt the soul.

This Feast of Unleavened Bread celebrated the beginning of the grain harvest which fifty days later culminated in the Pentecost or the Feast of Weeks. These festal observances become a parable of the soul. Christ woul lead us from the Passover deliverance to the Pentecostal dynamic. Through the indwelling and ministry of the Holy Spirit, He would make our lives fruitful for Him.

Great sacrificial Lamb of God, I thank You for the salvation and security in Your blood shed for me.

Portrait 38

Rock

... they drank of that spiritual Rock that followed them: and that Rock was Christ.

1 Corinthians 10:4

This text refers to the wilderness experience of the Hebrews when twice from the smitten rock there was the gushing forth of water to sustain and refresh them in an arid place. This occurred at Rephidim (Exodus 17:1–6), which was the beginning of the Exodus, and at Kadesh (Numbers 20:7–11), which was near the end of the Exodus wanderings. Paul indicates that the rock smitten by Moses was a prototype of Christ. Spiritualizing the historical experience he states, "that Rock was Christ": it was emblematic of what He did for us.

In the passage of Exodus 17 we read, ". . . the children of Israel journeyed from the wilderness of Sin . . . and there was no water for the people to drink." Man in his journey through the "wilderness of sin" finds life spiritually arid and needs the sustaining and refreshing water of life that Christ alone can give. As the Israelites were revived and refreshed by God's supernatural provision, so man's soul is revived and refreshed by the provision Christ our spiritual Rock has made for us.

But the rock had to be smitten in order to give forth the refreshing stream of water. Christ, our spiritual Rock, had to be smitten in order for us to partake of the life-giving stream that flows from His cross. Without His stripes we would have no healing, without His sorrows we would have no balm, without His thorns we would have no crown, without His wounds we would have no healing, without His death we would have no life. He is the "Rock of Ages" who was cleft for each of us.

This allegorical title for Christ has captured the imagination of other inspired hymn writers who have given us expressions that will live on in the songs of Christendom: "On Christ the solid rock, I stand" by Edward Mote; "Be our rock, our shield, our tower" by William Pearson; "We have an anchor . . . fastened to the Rock which cannot move" by Priscilla J. Owens; "He hideth my soul in the cleft of the rock" by Fanny Crosby.

The rock has been the symbol of strength and endurance. Of Him the Christian declares in confident testimony: "Thou art my Rock and my fortress" (Psalms 71:3).

In the Rocky Mountains, there is a train tunnel cut through solid rock and of such size that if two trains were passing each other there would be no room for a person in the tunnel. However there are two niches cut in the rock where a person may be safe. A sister and her little brother were caught in the tunnel one day with two trains approaching. She placed her little brother in one niche and then went to the one on the other side. Just as the trains were about to streak by she cried out, "Cling close to the rock." The trains passed and they were safe because they were in the clefts of the rock. So will we be safe amid the perils of life if we cling close to the Rock of Ages. As one person said, we may tremble on the Rock, but the Rock will never tremble under us.

Thou Rock of Ages, with the Psalmist I would pray, "Lead me to the rock that is higher than I." Help me to avoid the sinking sands of life and to build on Thee, who alone art the solid foundation.

Portrait 39

The Last Adam

... The first man Adam was made a living soul; the last Adam was made a quickening spirit.

1 Corinthians 15:45

This verse is part of that great Pauline chapter on the Resurrection. Paul is employing contrasts to drive home his thought. The word *first* prepares the reader for the climactic sequence to follow the word *last*.

Paul here portrays Christ as the "last Adam" and contrasts Him with the "first Adam." The English translations give a clue to the distinctions between the two kinds of life and the first and last Adam represent:

TRANSLATION	FIRST ADAM	LAST ADAM
KJV	living soul	quickening spirit
RSV	living being	life-giving spirit
NEB	an animate being	life-giving spirit
ANT	individual personality	restoring the dead to life

Paul says here that as Adam was the inaugurator of humanity (by divine fiat), so Christ was the inaugurator of eternal life. As Adam was the progenitor of everyman's humanity, so Christ is the progenitor of our spiritual sonship.

Adam represents for us *psyche*. Christ represents for us *pneuma*—the higher form of life. He indeed heightens as well the *psyche*—the human aspect of our life. But He imparts His Resurrection power and raises life to the dimension of eternity.

The first Adam brought death. This portrait of Christ as the Last Adam represents Him bringing eternal life. He gives us His power for our weakness, His glory for our dishonor, His incorruption for our corruption, His celestial life for our terrestrial existence, His *pneuma* for our *psyche*—His higher life for our lower life.

O Christ, Conqueror of death, raise me with You to the resurrection and radiance of life divine.

Portrait 40

Chief Corner Stone

... Jesus Christ himself being the chief corner stone.

Ephesians 2:20

Paul employs this architectural metaphor to indicate the relationship of Christ to His church and the believer. Christ spoke of Himself as a temple and referred to the temple He would build made without hands (*see* Mark 14:58). He is the rejected stone that became the head stone of the corner as spoken of by the Psalmist (*see* Psalms 118:22). This metaphor conveys several significant aspects of Christ's ministry relative to His holy temple composed of the "living stones" of His believers.

A cornerstone would control the design of an edifice. From that point, an architect would plan and relate the balance of the structure. Christ as the Chief Corner Stone should determine the direction and design of our lives. He will give symmetry to life. A life that is linked to Him will be enhanced and ennobled. He will make all the parts of life contribute to the whole. He will help us maintain the many facets of life in proper proportion and perspective.

Another function of the cornerstone was to unite. One of the definitions of a cornerstone is a "stone which lies at the corner of two walls, serving to unite them." Paul writes of the Chief Corner Stone, "In Him the whole structure is joined (bound, welded) together harmoniously" (Ephesians 2:21 AMPLIFIED NEW TESTAMENT). Christ imparts a cohesiveness to the Christian community. We are the "living stones" of His holy temple that are united to Him and to each other.

The cornerstone holds the most honored position. Peter wrote: "Unto you therefore which believe he is precious" (1 Peter 2:7). The word *precious* equates with *honor*. The cornerstone is the ceremonial block that is placed ritually in the outer wall bearing an inscription that memorializes the event and significant facts associated with the structure. Often the brick is hollow and is a repository of documents that will have future historical interest. This custom supposedly dates back over fifty centuries. The cornerstone held the most honored position in a structure. So the Chief Corner Stone holds the most honored position in a Christian's life—in our hearts, in our homes, and in our hopes.

The cornerstone was indispensable to the great Temple of Solomon. The words of our text, "I lay in Sion a chief corner stone," call to mind an interesting aspect of the Temple construction. The top plateau of Mount Moriah was not level or large enough for the total space required by the resplendent Temple. Thus the Israelites ingeniously constructed a large cornerpiece of heavy masonry that reached up from the plunging valley below and with this held up part of the illustrious Temple. To an observer it would seem as though that cornerpiece was holding up the Temple. We would be God's holy temple, sacred and indwelt by His Spirit. Our lives are quarried from a natural rock which of itself is not sufficient. But our sufficiency and our completeness come from the upholding power and presence of the Chief Corner Stone. From Him, our life derives its strength and support.

O Christ, be the cornerstone of my thought, my deeds, my life. Then will it have spiritual symmetry and significance.

Portrait 41

The Head of the Church

. . . Christ is the head of the church.

Ephesians 5:23

Paul, in Ephesians 1:19-23, writes of the ascended and exalted Christ enthroned at the right hand of God and dwelling in heavenly places in universal conquest. The culminating thought is, "gave him to be the head over all things to the church, Which is his body, the fulness of him that filleth all in all." Paul uses a physiological metaphor to express a stupendous thought—Christ is the head and the church is the body.

What is the church? It was once my privilege to tour some of the world's great cathedrals. One is greatly enriched by visiting the renowned cathedrals of Rome with their sacred history and graced by the works of some of the world's greatest artists and sculptors. In addition to the great cathedrals of Rome, the Quo Vadis Chapel on the Appian Way speaks volumes to the heart of the spiritually sensitive tourist. In Paris, Notre Dame has a mystical quality all its own. Majestic St. Paul's in London strikes many responsive chords in the heart of the visitor. At St. Giles in Edinburgh, one can imagine John Knox thundering forth his reformation sermons amidst the great Gothic pillars. Perhaps our most deeply stirring experience was the visit to the new cathedral at Coventry, replacing the one bombed in the blitz of the war. Its contemporary architecture and modern programs eloquently proclaim the Christian faith.

But these edifices with their worshipful features, and their unique spiritual aesthetics, as superb as they are, do not comprise in themselves the church. The sacerdotalism that characterizes these churches, the denominations they represent, are not the church in the ultimate sense. The church is something bigger, more vibrant than all these things. It is more than a cathedral or an organization.

A watch is an organization. It is made up of many parts all functioning in coordination in its intricate mechanism. But it is inanimate. The body also has a coordinating function. However it is more than an organization, it is an organism. Each part is alive and mutually dependent and contributing. So the church is a living organism. Christ is its Head. The company of believers is the body.

As the Head of the church, Christ is its leader and its authority. His presence rules its policy and its practice. As the Living Head His presence is realized by those who enter into the corporate experience of worship.

The phone of a church in Washington rang and an eager voice enquired, "Do you expect the president to be in church tomorrow?" The answer, "Not sure. But we expect Christ to be here and that is a reasonable incentive to bring a large congregation of people." Only when the presence of Christ is realized and He is truly the Head, do we have, in actuality, the true church.

The Scripture gives us a related discourse on the church with St. Paul using a nuptial symbol in designating the church as the Bride of Christ (*see* Ephesians 5:23-33). Marriage implies a sacred union. Thus is symbolized the sacred union between Christ and His followers. Marriage requires a mutual fidelity. Christ cannot and will not be faithless to us. May we be faithful to Him. Marriage involves a sacrifice: "Christ also loved the church, and gave himself for it." Have we made the sacrifice of ourselves to the claims of His great love?

O Christ, who gave Yourself in love for the church, help me to be a faithful member of the body of believers that acknowledge You as its exalted Head.

Portrait 42

Lord

And that every tongue should confess that Jesus Christ is Lord, to the glory of God the Father.

Philippians 2:11

This is one of the most common titles for Christ. Its application to Christ had a gradual growth until by the time Paul wrote his epistles he uses this title over two hundred times. It had both a human and a divine connotation, the latter becoming more pronounced following the Resurrection. It is probably the most theologically significant of all the titles of Christ.

The Greek-English Lexicon of W.F. Arndt and F.W. Gingrich suggests at least eight usages of this very sacred and significant title, *kurios.*

1. *Kurios* denoted the *owner* of possessions such as the owner of the vineyard (*see* Matthew 20:8) or the master of the house (*see* Mark 13:35).

As the Lord of the universe, "He has the whole world in His hands." The infinite depth of the universe is His habitation. This pygmy planet is just a speck in the universe of His green footstool. The imagination is staggered at the thought of His proprietorship in the cosmos. Yet, wonder of wonders, He holds my life in His mighty hands. The Lord of the universe is the Lord of my life.

2. This title also speaks of the *authority* of Jesus Christ. With the voice of authority, He commanded the raging wind and waves to be still. With the voice of authority, He brought forth Lazarus from his tomb of death. He demonstrated His authority over death and the grave by the mighty act of His Resurrection. It is sometimes said of restless youth today that they need the security of authority and discipline. In the authority of Jesus Christ there is security for the soul and its commitment.

3. *Kurios* was often used as an opposite to *doulos* or slave. Paul referred to himself as a "servant of Jesus Christ." But it was a joyful status. The paradox of the Christian life is that only when we become His servant do we have freedom, only when we surrender do we have victory, only when we die to self do we find life.

4. This title was also the designation of any person of high position.

It was my privilege to make a personal pilgrimage, as have so many others, to Stratford-on-Avon. There, one is inspired by the thought of a man who, writing with a whittled quill by the light of a tallow candle, produced lines that will be read and spoken until the end of time. If Shakespeare were to walk into any room today, everyone would stand up. But if Jesus Christ were to walk into a room, everyone would kneel. He towers above all other personages as the Peerless One of history.

5. *Kurios* was also used as a title for other supernatural beings (*see* Acts 10:4). We know not what other forms of beings exist in God's world, but the Bible does tantalize our imagination with hints of otherworldly life. All other celestial beings are but His couriers and are under His universal Lordship.

6. *Kurios* was also applied to *deified rulers* (*see* Acts 25:26), and

in particular, to later Roman emperors. But their glory was short-lived. Their claims were an illusion. Christ alone was great and big enough to fill this title.

7. Most important of all, *kurios* was a designation for *God* (*see* Matthew 5:33). It was the Greek translation of the sacred name Jehovah or Yahweh in the Old Testament. Thus, this title following His Resurrection had a tremendous significance when applied to Christ. It equates Him to a member of the Godhead. It is a recognition of His divinity.

8. "Jesus is *Kurios*" became the confession of the (Pauline) Christian church: "That if thou shalt confess with thy mouth the Lord Jesus . . . thou shalt be saved" (Romans 10:9). "And that every tongue should confess that Jesus Christ is Lord, to the glory of God the Father" (Philippians 2:11). The creed of the early church was not a what but a whom.

Infinite Christ, I would crown You Lord of my life, Lord of all.

Portrait 43

Image of the Invisible God

Who is the image of the invisible God. . . .

Colossians 1:15

In the title verse above, the Greek word *eikon* (translated *image*) had a rich association in the New Testament world. It is one of those words difficult to translate from the Greek, not having an English equivalent. It is also the word employed in 2 Corinthians 4:4 where Christ is spoken of as the "image of God." Although it does connote likeness its meaning goes beyond that. It means more than an accidental similarity such as one person to another. It represents more than an artificial imitation. It implies an original or an archetype from which the image is drawn.

All students of this text are deeply indebted to Bishop Lightfoot's incisive commentary on it. He writes, "Beyond the very obvious notion of likeness, the word for image involves the idea of representation and manifestation."

Thus Christ as the Image of God is the representation of God. He possessed all the essential qualities of deity. Just as upon analysis a tiny drop of the ocean has all the same elements of the vast ocean, so Christ in human form represented the essential characteristics of divinity. In Him we see the righteousness of God, the judgment of God, the purity of God, the character of God, the mighty love of God, the power of God.

Christ was the visible manifestation of the Invisible God. Jesus, in His revealing dialogue with Philip in the Upper Room said, ". . . he that hath seen Me hath seen the Father" (John 14:9). He was the Infinite Lord that had become the Intimate Life. He was the embodiment of deity. He was God in human flesh and form. He was God speaking the language of the man in the street. He was God in understandable terms.

When we think of God we think of Christ. He is our mental image and concept of what God is like. The imagination cannot frame a more noble picture, the intellect cannot conceive a higher concept, nor can the soul devise a more exalted image of God, than that He should be like Christ. He is God's self-disclosure.

There are two other titles closely related to this one. In Hebrews 1:3, Christ is called the "brightness of his glory." We cannot look directly at the brilliance of the noonday sun. But its rays and its warmth reveal to us what the sun is like. Christ was the ray that penetrated the earth's dark atmosphere and enabled men to see and know something of the glory and the effulgence of the Eternal Light.

In Hebrews 1:3, Christ is also called the "express image of his person." We have in the original text the interesting word *charakter* for *express image*. It was the word that described the impression of a seal left on wax or clay. Thus Jesus as the *charakter* of God is a faithful and detailed reproduction of the nature of God. In His life and ministry there was faithfully traced the character of deity.

Catherine Baird's words beautifully express in devotional words God as Love revealed in Christ:

> O Love, revealed on earth in Christ,
>   In blindness once I sacrificed
> Thy gifts for dress; I could not see,
>   But Jesus brings me sight of Thee.
>
> O Love, invisible before,
>   I see Thee now, desire Thee more;
> When Jesus speaks, Thy word is clear;
>   I search His face and find Thee near.

Eternal Christ, I thank You for making God real and known to me in history and in my heart.

Portrait 44

Firstborn of Every Creature

Who is . . . the firstborn of every creature.
                                    Colossians 1:15

In this great Christological passage, the word *firstborn* is translated from the Greek *prototokos*. The word portrays two transcendent aspects of Christ.

It suggests His preexistence, His eternity. He is the Unbeginning as well as the Unending One. He always was. Before the eons of time recorded in the geological strata of the earth, before the stars were set on their courses, Christ was. He is the Timeless One who holds all time in His hands. Our finite minds cannot grasp the infinite aspect of Christ. We just cannot conceive how Christ and God always were, having had no beginning. But then if the finite could comprehend the Infinite, the Infinite would be finite.

Edwin M. Stanton, Secretary of War, had been kneeling by the bedside of a gaunt, haggard figure. He arose in that historic moment as Lincoln expired and said, "Now he belongs to the ages." Those words have rung true through the succeeding years. In a far superior way are they true of Jesus Christ. He alone belongs to all the ages. Christ belongs to no particular age, no era or epoch. He is the Eternal One. His short sojourn on earth was but a moment, a minute fraction of time in His eternal existence.

This word *prototokos* also speaks of the priority and precedence of

Christ in all creation. The Hebrew equivalent of this term in the Old Testament is consistent with the precedence of the firstborn being destined as the heir and ruler (*see* Psalms 89:27).

Our concept of Christ must give Him precedence over all other things. St. Augustine wrote, "Christ is not valued at all unless He be valued above all." Someone else has said that Christ is not Lord at all unless He is Lord of all. To some people Jesus is nothing. To others, He is something. Then there are those to whom Jesus is Everything.

Eternal Christ, lift my life from its prison house of clay and time and link me with the eternal verities of Thy Kingdom.

Portrait 45

Mediator

> *For there is one God, and one mediator between God and men, the man Christ Jesus.*
>
> 1 Timothy 2:5

In New Testament times, a mediator or a *mesites* was commonly known among the people. He was the one who came between two parties who had a dispute or a difference. He was the middleman who would arbitrate between the separated and contesting parties or persons. Today the word *mediator* still means one who brings about an agreement between two parties at variance.

In the Old Testament, we hear the plaintive cry of Job, "Neither is there any daysman betwixt us" (Job 9:33). The word *daysman* in the Septuagint is the same word of our text translated *mediator*. Job in his desperate crisis longed for someone who could mediate between him and God. Job's yearning had to go unsatisfied. But in Hebrews 12:24 Christ is called the Mediator of the New Covenant. In our text, Paul declares that Christ is the only Mediator between God and men.

Christ fulfilled two vital functions as Mediator. A mediator has to be able to *represent* both parties. Christ represented both God and man. He represented God as a member of the Godhead. He alone was able to represent the Cosmic Presence. Because He had come from the courts of God, He could represent the eternal council of God.

The miracle of the Incarnation also qualified Him to represent man. He was clothed in the garb of humanity. He carried man's burdens, endured man's agony, suffered man's sorrows, was tested by man's trials and temptations, lived as a man among men, and died a man's death. He was the Infinite who had become the Intimate, the Divine Sovereign who became the human sufferer. Thus He was able to represent man.

A mediator also has the task of *reconciliation*. This was the second vital function of Christ as Mediator. God did not need to be reconciled to man. God has always been seeking man out. He is the Eternal Lover of man's soul. He is the Hound of Heaven who has ever been pursuing man to restore the broken relationship. Man is the renegade. Man is the one who has been disloyal to the love and fellowship of God. Jesus' role as Mediator is to bring man back into the relationship God has for him.

There was only one way He could effect this reconciliation. That was the awful price of the cross. Man's rebellion had stamped upon it the penalty of eternal death. God in His righteousness decreed that without the shedding of blood there would be no remission of sin. Thus, the way of the cross was the only way to reconciliation. The cross was the great bridge from earth to heaven. It spanned the deep chasm of sin. It is the place where the broken relationship is restored. ". . . God was in Christ, reconciling the world unto himself" (2 Corinthians 5:19).

Thou Divine Mediator, keep me in fellowship and faith with my Creator.

Portrait 46

The King of Kings

... who is the blessed and only Potentate, the King of kings, and Lord of lords.

1 Timothy 6:15

Paul calls forth his highest superlatives to try to describe and define Jesus Christ. Compared to the brightness of His majesty all other kings are only as smoking flax vainly endeavoring to illuminate the noontide.

Shelley, in one of his sonnets, speaks of meeting a traveler from Egypt. In the desert, the traveler had found the remains of a statue, with two trunkless legs, and near them a broken face. On the pedestal was this inscription:

> My name is Ozymandias, king of kings:
> Look on my works, ye Mighty, and despair!

Ozymandias had the effrontery to style himself "king of kings", but he left behind him only a couple of legs and a broken visage in stone.

Jesus in His unapproachable glory as King of kings left behind Him an eternal kingdom. Let us consider certain aspects of His Kingship.

Every King must have a *right to the title.* Not just anyone can set himself up as king. The universal requirement for kingship has been royal blood. There must be royal blood coursing through the veins of the one who would ascend the throne. Earth's monarchies and dynasties have had a succession by royal lineage.

Matthew, the genealogist, carefully traces the Davidic descent of Jesus. To many minds, it was necessary to certify in this manner the Messiahship of Jesus. However great was Christ's descent from Israel's illustrious king, His title to Kingship does not rest upon such an earthly and decaying foundation. Jesus is the King of kings not because He was the son of David but because He was and is the Son of God. His Kingship rests upon the eternal foundation of His divinity. His divine right was based upon His divine character.

Every king has a *throne.* In the part of majestic Westminister Abbey known as St. Edward's Chapel, there is what many consider to be England's most precious relic, the ancient Coronation Chair. It dates from the time of Edward I in 1300 and has been used for every coronation since that time. It was made to hold the historic Stone of Scone which is in repose at the base of the chair. As I looked upon that chair, my imagination suddenly came under the spell of the illustrious array of queens and kings who sat upon that throne in their brief moment of glory and grandeur.

What about the throne of the King of kings? Is there no throne of grandeur for the Lord of the Universe? The Scripture gives us our answer: ". . . heaven . . . is God's throne" (Matthew 5:34). "Jesus . . . is set down at the right hand of the throne of God" (Hebrews 12:2). Jesus today reigns from the celestial, unfading, eternal throne of God in Heaven.

There is another throne that needs to come under the Lordship of Jesus Christ. It is the throne from which there issues all the orders of life—the throne of the human heart. Does He reign without a rival on the throne of your heart?

Every king has *power.* Jesus alone could make the claim, "All power is given unto me in heaven and in earth" (Matthew 28:18).

Every king has *subjects and a kingdom.* Jesus said, "My kingdom is not of this world" (John 18:36). While other kingdoms fade and vanish, the eternal Kingdom of Jesus Christ continues to expand.

Many have given their lives at the command of an earthly king. Have you given your heart, your life to Jesus—the King of kings, the blessed and only Potentate, and Lord of lords?

Lord of lords, and King of kings, rule supremely upon the throne of my life.

Portrait 47

Heir of All Things

Hath in these last days spoken unto us by his Son, whom he hath appointed heir of all things, by whom also he made the worlds.

Hebrews 1:2

The grandeur and the glory of this title are unfathomable to human and finite minds. The inheritance of Christ has no qualification or restriction whatsoever. He is the Heir of All Things.

This verse has a companion text: "The kingdoms of this world are become the kingdoms of our Lord, and of his Christ: and he shall reign for ever and ever" (Revelation 11:15). These words from the great seer's rapturous vision speak of the eschatological kingdom and glory of our Lord which is too often lost in contemporary Christianity. It was the assurance of this truth that sustained the martyrs in their hour of testing and tragedy. It is the truth that can give new life and incentive to our evangelistic thrust of today. There will be a great Coronation Day for the One who is the Lord of lords and the King of kings. Then this world will become His Kingdom. It will be an eternal kingdom of peace, righteousness, and unspeakable joy.

By what right does Christ become Heir of All Things? Our text declares first of all that it is by the *right of relationship*. He is the Son of God. The word *heir* as a legal term refers to one who comes to an inheritance by natural right rather than by a will. Under our intestacy laws, where a person of wealth dies without a formal will, the inheritance is often determined by a degree of consanguinity or blood relationship. The nearest of kin is given precedence. Christ's unique relationship to God as His Son gives Him natural right to all of God's universe.

Secondly, Christ becomes Heir by *divine appointment*. God has appointed Christ as Heir. Thus Christ's right to the inheritance is incontestable and incontrovertible. God's sovereignty in the universe cannot be challenged. The creature cannot dispute with the Creator. Man is but the lessee of God's gracious benefits. God is the Cosmic Legator. In more ways than we can ever even be aware, we are beneficiaries of the Universal Benefactor. In the end "all things" will become the inheritance of Christ.

Christ also has His right of the inheritance of the cosmos derived from *His own supremacy*. Our verse states that Christ was an agent of the creation. This truth is revealed in other passages of Scripture as well. Thus His is the right of the Creator. To a creator belongs that which he brings into existence.

There is another glorious truth of Scripture related to this great title: "The Spirit itself beareth witness with our spirit, that we are the children of God: And if children, then heirs; heirs of God, and jointheirs with Christ; if so be that we suffer with him, that we may be also glorified together" (Romans 8:16,17). Hallelujah! He shares His inheritance with us! Mansions of glory, life that shall endless be, worlds unknown, knowledge now unimaginable, eternal fellowship with God —all this and more than we can begin to conceive. "Eye hath not seen, nor ear heard, neither have entered into the heart of man, the things which God hath prepared for them that love him" (1 Corinthians 2:9).

A story is told of Theodore Roosevelt boarding ship at an African port as he was to return from a hunting safari. Great crowds gathered and celebrated his visit. The red carpet was rolled out for him. He was given the best suite on board the ship. He was the center of attention during the sail home. At the same time, there was another man on board ship. He was an old missionary who had given his life for God in Africa. His wife had died, his children gone, he was now alone. No one noticed him. At the ship's arrival in San Francisco, the president was again feted. The whistles blew, the bells rang, the crowds cheered as Roosevelt disembarked in pomp and glory. But there was no one there to meet the missionary. He went to a small hotel room and that night as he knelt beside his bed he prayed, "I'm not complaining, Lord. But I just don't understand. I gave my life for You in Africa and it seems that no one cares. I just don't understand." And then it seemed in that moment, the Lord reached down His hand from Heaven and placing it upon the old man's shoulder, said, "Missionary, you're not home yet."

Eternal Christ, my imagination and mind reel at the thought of Thy infinite love. Thy love claims and receives what little I give in return.

Portrait 48

Apostle of Our Profession

> ... Consider the Apostle ... of our profession, Christ Jesus.
>
> Hebrews 3:1

Apostle means the one sent. This title implies a direct commission from God to man. There were other apostles, but Jesus was sent of God in a way unlike that of any other.

This title suggests two things about Christ. He was sent. We ask, "By whom?" Thus the title suggests the *Person* who sent Him. Divine imprimatur was upon His mission. "God was in Christ."

In the fourth Gospel, Jesus twenty-six times uses the expression, "He who sent me." He also uses a synonymous verb eighteen times in reference to His mission from the Father.

This term does not detract from the voluntariness of Jesus' coming. Jesus said, "I lay down my life.... No man taketh it from me, but I lay it down of myself" (John 10:17,18). His compulsion was His compassion.

This word *apostle* poses a second question. He was sent. For what *purpose?* Why?

His Advent was not an emergency measure of God to meet a sudden calamity. Before time commenced its solemn march, God's love anticipated man's need. We read in Revelation 13:8 that Jesus is the "... Lamb slain from the foundation of the world." Christ's redemptive mission was not an afterthought of God, but was pre-arranged in the councils of eternity. God is omniscient. He is prescient. He foreknows and foresees the future. Christ was sent as an Apostle by God. His mission was determined and dedicated before the creation of our world, before Adam and Eve, before the Fall.

We read in Philippians 2:7 that "[He] made himself of no reputation, and took upon him the form of a servant." The servant's role was voluntarily assumed to accomplish the great work of redemption. No theologian can fathom the mystery and majesty of Christ's renunciation to become a servant. No mystic can plumb its depths of devotion. Christ went from riches to rags that we might go from rags to riches. He became bankrupt that we might inherit His imperishable riches. He descended the steps of glory that we might ascend with Him to worlds unknown. He became a pauper that we might become princes. He became what we were that He might make us what He is.

Does not this title suggest another scriptural truth for our consideration? Jesus said to His followers, ". . . as my Father hath sent me, even so send I you" (John 20:21). Christ was an Apostle, sent by God the Father to men. Now, in His physical absence from this world, He depends on us to make known God's Word and will to men. Will you be as *one sent* by the Master? Will you accept the challenge?

Thank You, Christ, for coming to this troubled and tortured world. Let not Your sacrifice for me be lost and let not Your image in me die. Help me to go and tell the immortal message.

Portrait 49

The Pioneer of Our Faith

> Looking to Jesus the pioneer . . . of our faith. . . .
> Hebrews 12:2 RSV

The Greek word applied to Christ in this verse had a many-splendored association. This word, *archegon,* is made up of *age* meaning to lead, and *arche* meaning the first. Thus, this compound word means the chief leader or one who takes the lead in something and thus provides an example. This word is variously translated as Prince, Captain, Author, Leader, Chief Leader, Guide, Source, Prince Leader.

Perhaps the word *Pioneer* translates its meaning best in representing Christ as the One who has gone ahead and blazed the trail for us to follow. He is our great Trailblazer who has gone on in the way that was previously untrod. He has opened for us new frontiers and new worlds which beckon us to follow in the trail He has blazed.

As the Pioneer of our Faith, He has opened for us the path that leads to abundant, vibrant, victorious, fulfilling, and eternal life. He leads us forth from the hinterlands of mere existence to the frontiers of exciting discoveries and delights. Following in His footsteps, we are led to the high plateaus where we find true perspective and purpose.

In Hebrews 2:10 (RSV), Christ is portrayed as the *Archegon* or Pioneer of our salvation. His path led to the agonies suffered in the shadows of Gethsemane. He trod in deep sorrow the Via Dolorosa. He trekked up the lonely and tortuous path that led to Calvary. He traveled down the dark and desolate road that led to our salvation.

But He returned with the gleaming keys of salvation and eternal life at His side. He opened for us the doors to heaven.

The final in this trilogy of texts employing this rich word, *Archegon*, portrays Christ as the "pioneer . . . of our faith" (Hebrews 12:1 RSV). In the preceding chapter, Paul has just given the Roll Call of Faith in this Westminster Abbey of the Bible. Christ is the Chief Leader of our faith. We need to keep our eyes fixed on the Pioneer of Our Faith in order to avoid the distractions and detours that will prevent us from reaching our goal in the great race of life.

This last text gives us a compound title: "The pioneer and perfecter of our faith." He who has originated, authored, and pioneered our faith will also perfect it. He has not deserted life's path and those who travel upon it. His presence and His resources enable us to go all the way with Him to fulfill life's ultimate design and reach life's ultimate destination.

O Christ, the Pioneer of the way that lies before me, give me endurance to follow You all the way.

Portrait 50

High Priest

Whither the forerunner is for us entered, even Jesus, made an high priest for ever after the order of Melchisedec.

Hebrews 6:20

Christ was, on our behalf, a Forerunner, one who went before us. But where? The word *whither* traces from the preceding verses the place—"within the veil." It is referring to the Holy of Holies which represented the very presence of God. Previously only the high priest of the Aaronic order could go into the Holy of Holies, and he but once a year. He went as the representative of the people. They could not go after him, but Christ went as the Forerunner and opened a direct access to God for us. No longer is there required a human intermediary. The veil was rent in two. The middle wall of partition was broken down. Christ as our Forerunner conferred the sacred privilege of the priesthood on all believers.

The writer declares that Christ is a High Priest of a new and different order from that of the sacerdotal system of the Levites. He is of the order of Melchizedek. The name slips into the Bible narrative in Genesis 14:17–20. In Hebrews 7, the superiority of Melchizedek is delineated by Abraham's payment of tithes to him. This placed the great patriarch in an inferior position to Melchizedek. The Psalmist prophesied of the Messiah: "Thou art a priest for ever after the order of Melchizedek" (110:4). Thus was Melchizedek a prototype of the Great High Priest who was yet to come.

Melchizedek had *no recorded beginning or ending*. Thus is symbolized the eternal priesthood of Christ. Other priests held their office for only a transient period and then would be succeeded by another. But Christ's was a perpetual priesthood.

Melchizedek had *no recorded parents*. The record of parentage was the *sine qua non* for the Levitical priest. His ancestry was the primary criterion for his office. But Melchizedek was not a priest by pedigree. Neither was Christ a priest by descent from the tribe of Levi. He was of the tribe of Judah and represented a new and higher order of priesthood.

The name Melchizedek meant King of Righteousness. He was also the King of Salem which meant peace. Christ is also the King of Righteousness and the King of Peace. These two great qualities will characterize the new Kingdom He will usher in when He returns to take His Kingdom and His crown.

One of the primary functions of the high priest was intercession for the people. On his shoulders were two onyx stones with the names of the twelve tribes inscribed on them. Also upon his breastplate were twelve stones with the names of the twelve tribes. Thus was Israel represented upon the shoulders of his strength and the heart of his love. Christ, our Great High Priest, upon the shoulders of His omnipotence and upon His heart of infinite love carries our names and our needs into the presence of God. ". . . he ever liveth to make intercession for them" (Hebrews 7:25).

Christ is our Great High Priest by the efficacy of His atoning sacrifice. In Hebrews 9:4, there is described the furnishings of the Holy of Holies: the golden censer, the Ark of the Covenant overlaid with gold containing the golden pot that had manna, and Aaron's rod that budded, and the Ten Commandments. But there is one piece of furniture that significantly was not included. That was a chair—for the work of the high priest was never finished. Year after year, on the Great Day of Atonement, he would again have to enter the Holy of Holies and offer his sacrifice. However, we read of Christ and His sacrificial work, "But this man, after he had offered one sacrifice for sins for ever, sat down on the right hand of God" (Hebrews 10:12). He alone could say of His priestly work of atonement, "It is finished."

Our scriptural context also declares the extent of His atoning work: "Wherefore he is able also to save them to the uttermost that come unto God by him" (Hebrews 7:25).

O Christ, my Great High Priest, I thank Thee for opening the new and living way unto God for me.

Portrait 51

Advocate

And if any man sin, we have an advocate with the Father, Jesus Christ the righteous.

1 John 2:1

The word *sin* here is in the aorist tense in the Greek and refers to a sin that has been done in the past in contrast to the present tense which would represent habitual sinning. If we are sorry for a sin we have done and are willing to renounce it, we have an Advocate who will help us to receive forgiveness.

The word *advocate* here is the Greek word *parakletos* which John also uses in the 14th, 15th, and 16th chapters of his Gospel as a term for the Holy Spirit. However, there Jesus applies this word to Himself as well by saying, "I will send you another to be your Advocate [Paraclete]" (John 14:15,16 NEB). The word means one called alongside to help, one to plead our cause, which is the rendering of the New English Bible for this text.

The Holy Spirit as *Paraclete* can do many things for us. He convicts, regenerates or brings about the new birth, empowers, guides, purifies, helps us in our praying. But there is one thing the Holy Spirit cannot do for us. He cannot acquit us from our guilt of sin. Jesus Christ alone can be our Advocate, our *Paraclete,* in achieving our pardon in the divine court of justice.

In the time when this Scripture was written, the word translated *Advocate* referred to one who took one's side in a trial. There is a divine law that has been broken. God's Law declares, "the soul that sinneth, it shall die" (Ezekiel 18:20). We have all sinned and come under the condemnation of that law. We are guilty. We are under the death sentence. What can we do?

We have an Advocate—One who pleads our cause. He intercedes on our behalf. Not to prove our innocence, for we are guilty. We have grieved Him by a thousand falls, but we have an Advocate who stands on our behalf at the bar of divine justice:

Jesus—His human name as part of this text, reminds us of His understanding of our frailties and failures;

Christ—He is God's anointed. He has a unique standing with God the Father and will have the attention of the Divine Judge;

The Righteous—He has the moral qualifications fitting Him to be the Mediator between man and God.

O Christ, my Advocate with the Father, thank You for pleading my cause. By the merit of Your sacrifice, may I have pardon, and by the cleansing of Your Spirit, may I have purity.

Portrait 52

Lion of the Tribe of Judah

> ... *Weep not: behold, the Lion of the Tribe of Juda, the Root of David, hath prevailed.* . . .
>
> Revelation 5:5

The inspired seer has a strange juxtaposition of metaphors for Christ. In our text He is called the Lion and in the very next verse He is called the Lamb. Have we encountered an incompatibility in our study of the titles of Christ? Can Christ the Lamb and Christ the Lion be reconciled?

Upon consideration, we see that both portraits are essential to Christ and His ministry. The figure of the Lamb represents His suffering and sacrifice for us. We also need the figure of the Lion that represents His conquest in His suffering and offering. The sacrifice without the conquest would have been just another in the long succession of martyrdoms in the history of man.

The Amplified New Testament vividly renders this verse, "Stop weeping! See, the Lion of the tribe of Judah . . . has won—has overcome and conquered!" Today there is much lamentation over the problems and perplexities of man. Is not our text apposite in that it says to us, "Stop lamenting—look to Christ who is the Mighty Conqueror!" Our world is not so much helped by those who say, "Look what the world has come to" as it is by those who declare, "Look what has come to the world!"

In our day of crises and chaos, we need to behold this portrait of Christ the Conqueror. Let us do away with the pictures and concepts of an anemic Christ. We need to see Christ the Lion—Christ the Invincible Conqueror for our times. Let us behold His blazing wrath over injustice, war, violence, evil. Let us see Him as the One who will come in the role of the Mighty Conqueror.

Let us find in Him our concepts that will, when linked with our action, bring remedial measures to the ills of life. Let us find in Him our strength to attack the injustices that assail the dignity and worth of man.

The succeeding chapter deals with catastrophes of life that emanated from the opening of the seals. They represent a catalog of some of the worst disasters than can assault life: war, mourning and distress, the pale horse of death, persecution, calamities of a convulsive nature. Yet, in view of all these distresses and seeming disasters, Christ is portrayed as the Conqueror. He is the Master of the storm. He can guide our frail lifeboat to its haven.

While camping in Algonquin Park, Canada, one summer, one of our girls, quite young at the time, was sure she could climb a mountain trail with us. Her eagerness was too sweet to resist and so we allowed her to come with the two older children as we started our climb up Lookout Trail. She danced ahead, confident of her strength. Soon the road became a trail, and soon the trail became frowning rocks. Finally, she sat down, exhausted. Then her father reached out his arm, and, taking hold of it, she reached the summit, that would not have been possible in her own strength alone.

Life is an uphill path. It, too, has its precipices and frowning rocks and steep ascents. But Christ conquered for us and He will take our hands and guide us safely to the end of life's journey.

O Christ, Mighty Conqueror, enable me to ride masterfully on the sea of life.

One of the best ways to gain a deeper understanding of the nature of Jesus Christ is to study the names and titles used to refer to Him in Scripture. Each name—from the simplest to the most poetic, reveals a unique aspect of Jesus' character and contributes to an accurate portrait of His person and His purpose.

PORTRAITS OF CHRIST contains fifty-two illuminating devotional studies of names and titles given to Jesus Christ in the Old and New Testaments. The individual "portraits" are divided into four groups according to their Biblical context: The Prophecy — prophetically ascribed titles; The Advent — names associated with Jesus' coming; The Person — the "I ams" or self-ascribed titles; and The Ministry—names and titles associated with Jesus' life and work. Together, they cover the complete Biblical spectrum of references to Jesus.

Among the titles included are familiar ones such as Messiah, King, Good Shepherd, Lamb of God, Bread of Life, Alpha and Omega, as well as more obscure ones such as Shiloh, Rod and Branch, Horn of Salvation, Mediator, Chief Corner Stone, Lion of the Tribe of Judah. Each devotion begins with a Scripture quotation in which the particular name or title is mentioned, followed by a thorough explanation of its origin, its meaning and its significance. These fifty-two penetrating studies provide enlightening and inspiring material for personal study or weekly group devotions.